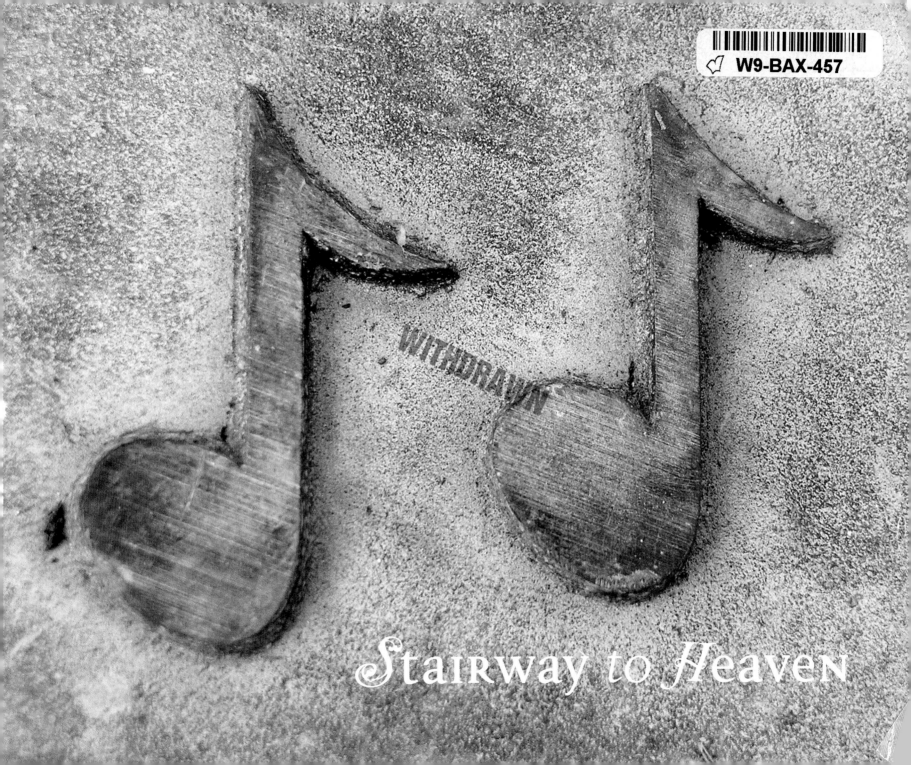

Stairway to Heaven

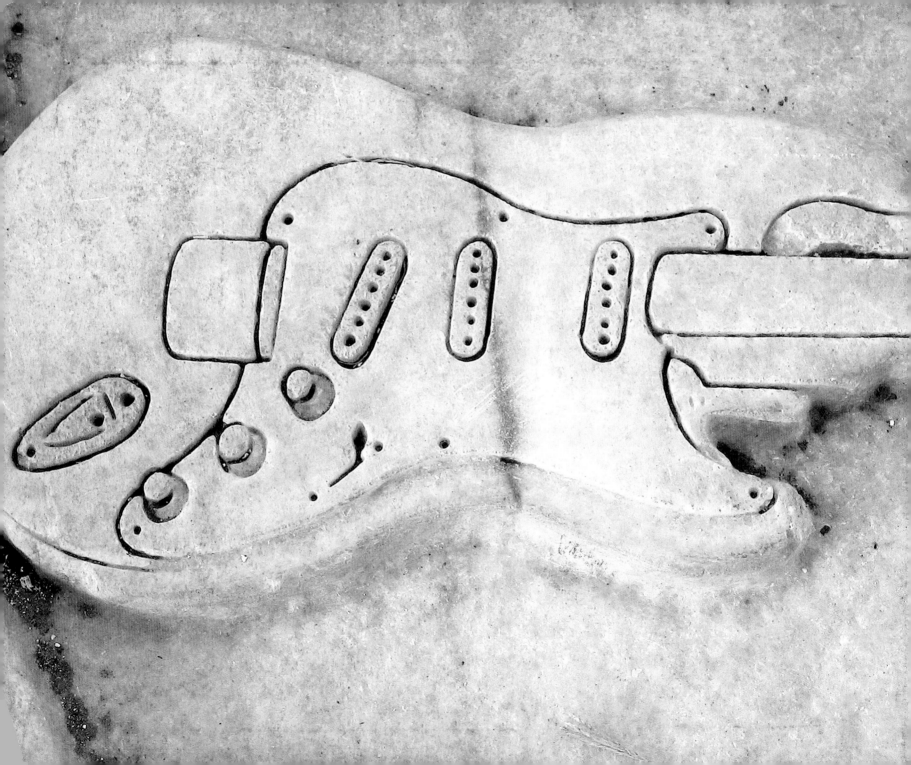

Stairway to Heaven

the final resting places of rock's legends

J.D. Reed
and
maddy miller

WENNER BOOKS NEW YORK

FRONT COVER: Photograph of Jim Morrison's grave at Père-Lachaise, Paris, France, by John Pearson Wright

BACK COVER: Photograph of George Harrison memorial at Strawberry Fields, Central Park, New York City, by Jen Lombardo

A Jackalope Press Production
Editorial Director: Holly George-Warren
Designer: Ellen Nygaard
Managing Editor: Nina Pearlman
Editorial Contributors: Robin Aigner, Rachel X. Weissman
Susan Gordon, Amy Blankstein, Mark Dorrity, Tom Fraser,
Viki Scholten

Wenner Books
Editor-in-Chief: Robert Wallace
Production Chief: John Dragonetti
Production Manager: KellyAnn S. Kwiatek
Editorial and Production Contributors: Kate Rockland, Linda Pitt

Reed, J. D., 1940-
  Stairway to heaven: the final resting places of rock's legends / [J. D. Reed ; Maddy Miller, photographer].
    p. cm. -- (Jd Reed)
  Includes bibliographical references and index.
  ISBN 1-932958-54-1
  1. Rock musicians--Tombs. 2. Rock musicians--Death. 3. Cemeteries--United States--Guidebooks. I. Miller, Maddy. II. Title. III. Series.
  ML385.R44 2005
  781.66'092'2--dc22
                    2005006081
ISBN: 1-932958-54-1

Wenner books are available for special promotions and premiums. For details contact Michael Rentas, Manager, Inventory and Premium Sales, Hyperion, 77 West 66th Street, 11th Floor, New York, NY 10023, or call 212-456-0133.

10 9 8 7 6 5 4 3 2 1

PAGE 1: *Detail from the tombstone of Mama Cass Elliot*
PAGE 2: *A carving of Buddy Holly's Stratocaster on his tombstone*
PAGE 3: *The grave of singer Bianca Halstead, Hollywood, California*
PAGE 5: *Drumsticks left at the grave of Led Zeppelin's John Bonham*

the tune will come to you at last
when all are one and one is all
to be a rock and not to roll

"stairway to heaven"
— jimmy page & robert plant

∽ contents ∽

OPPOSITE PAGE: *A detail from Lisa Lopes's grave, sprinkled with coins left by fans*

∽ Introduction ∽

At 7:30 a.m. on a sweltering July day, I climbed the curving driveway of Graceland, Elvis Presley's mansion/museum in Memphis, Tennessee. During business hours, only buses shuttling ticket holders are allowed up the drive. But for an hour or so in the early morning, the white wrought-iron gate swings open onto Elvis Presley Boulevard, allowing visitors, fans, and a few obsessives inside. Only one attraction is open that early: the emotional acme of the eighteen-dollar regular tour – Elvis's grave.

A dozen or so others made the trek with me, heading to the back of the house, its decor flash-frozen in 1977, when the King died at age forty-two. Near the swimming pool, Elvis, his parents, and his grandmother are buried in a semicircle under massive bronze slabs. At the foot of the markers blooms an odd little garden of intricate flower arrangements, colorful posters, notes in many languages, and a menagerie of teddy bears. One middle-age woman in our party wore a pink-and-black poodle skirt and saddle shoes; two young Japanese tourists sweltered under leather jackets as they shot video footage.

But the most galvanizing sight was a young woman in her early twenties sitting on the steps near the graves, weeping. It wasn't sniffles-and-a-tissue kind of crying. Her shoulders were heaving; the sobs came from the center of her being. The awkward young man accompanying her pulled his camouflage hunting cap low over his brow and stared into the distance, embarrassed. She was far too young to have seen Elvis when he was alive, or to have twirled in a high school gymnasium to "Heartbreak Hotel" and "Blue Suede Shoes." The music that moved her as a teen would have been R.E.M., Garth Brooks, or Madonna. But here she was, raw and wounded, pulled by some compulsion to the burial place of a man who would have been almost seventy had he lived.

What I witnessed happens thousands of times every day around the world – though usually with far less emotional affect. Fans visit the graves of musicians – both the celebrated and the obscure. More than six hundred thousand visitors file past Elvis's marker every year; Jim Morrison's tomb is one of the top five tourist attractions in Paris; and the foot traffic to Hank Williams's headstone is so heavy that the grass had to be replaced with artificial turf.

Stairway to Heaven is a celebration of this phenomenon. For my part, I wanted to explore the forces that draw us to these graves, as well as tell the

OPPOSITE PAGE: *Outside the gates of Graceland, August 17, 1977*

A painted rock at the grave of folkie Harry Chapin

tales about the musicians, their last moments, and their final resting places – in other words, what lies beneath the granite, the marble, and the bronze.

My coauthor, photographer and picture editor Maddy Miller, was way ahead of me. She had been photographing graves all over the world long before this project began, fascinated by the bucolic nature of cemeteries, the architecture of the headstones, and the curious mementos visitors leave behind. Her interest, and her eye, give *Stairway to Heaven* its power. The photographs, by Maddy and others, pay elegant tribute to this world of the departed and the surprising amount of activity that surrounds it. They catch details that evoke vital presences – a leather jacket hanging from the headstone of punk rocker Joey Ramone; a bouquet of drumsticks at the grave of Led Zeppelin stickman John Bonham; crystals and painted rocks left for folkie Harry Chapin; and in cemeteries across the country, thousands of guitar picks strewn like seeds.

Some of rock's greatest figures are not included here: They have no markers. Kurt Cobain, Tupac Shakur, Freddie Mercury, John Entwistle, Barry White, Marvin Gaye, Jeff Buckley, and dozens of others were cremated and their ashes either scattered or given to their families. Bobby Darin has no grave because he donated his body to the UCLA Medical School, and Screamin' Jay Hawkins, whose act involved climbing out of caskets as a rockin' ghoul, said he didn't want to be buried because he'd spent too much time in coffins while he was alive. Other rockers were cremated but are indelibly memorialized. John Lennon's Strawberry Fields in Manhattan's Central Park, for instance, has become a gathering spot to remember not only his death but those of others. Crowds gathered there when Jerry

Garcia died, and again when George Harrison passed away.

The diversity among rockers' resting places is remarkable. Some of the giants have the most understated graves; some of the least known, the most elaborate. Ray Charles's crypt in the wall of an L.A. mausoleum carries only a small G clef and his name, RAY CHARLES ROBINSON, while the burial of L.A. punk rocker Bianca Halstead, lead singer of the obscure group Betty Blowtorch, included putting her ashes in a Kiss lunchbox that was then placed in the kind of wheeled case roadies use to transport amplifiers.

The words carved on tombstones tell many tales. Some sentiments, for example, take us backstage. Artists, like most people, are usually sent on the last journey by their families, and their inscriptions reflect losses close to home. The gravestone of Jam Master Jay, for instance, reads BELOVED HUSBAND AND FATHER, not exactly the public image of the turntable genius of Run-D.M.C. The graves of other musicians take us back to their beginnings by bearing their birth names. For example, Howlin' Wolf lies in a Chicago cemetery as Chester A. Burnett. But, hey, it's rock & roll, and the irrepressible spirit of the music surrounds many memorials. The marker of Rob Tyner, frontman of the 1960s revolutionary MC5, reads LET ME BE WHO I AM, and the words of Righteous Brother Bobby Hatfield's headstone come from one of the duo's songs: IF YOU BELIEVE IN FOREVER . . . THEN LIFE IS JUST A ONE-NIGHT STAND.

Rock is barely a half-century old, and too many of its stars are already in cemeteries. Ritchie Valens ("La Bamba") was only seventeen and on the cusp of stardom when he was killed in a 1959 plane crash

Gene Vincent still rocks in this grave-marker portrait.

along with Buddy Holly and the Big Bopper. Jimi Hendrix, Janis Joplin, and Jim Morrison all died at twenty-seven – from alcohol and drugs. A few bands have suffered curses, too. Four of the five members of the classic Temptations lineup died before their time; much of Lynyrd Skynyrd went down in flames. Sex, drugs, burnout, and reckless-ness – also tragic car wrecks and plane crashes – can be blamed in the deaths of many musicians who died young. And when a rock star checks out early, it seems to legitimize his or her outlaw persona.

In a larger sense, the celebrity culture in which we bathe propels many fans to venerate stardom to even greater limits. "I would call celebrity worship a new form of religious culture," said Gary Laderman, a professor of religion at Emory University. Fans "may not even know the fallen celebrit[ies], yet they draw quite a bit of meaning from them." *Elvis never really left the building.*

Okay, enough Psych 101. What we know for sure is that searching out and visiting the graves of rock stars has become a consuming pastime for a growing number of fans. So many visitors ask for directions to the grave of AC/DC's Bon Scott, for instance, that Australia's sprawling Freemantle Cemetery has a map of the grounds with arrows to his grave taped to its office window. Many American cemeteries do the same, and so heavily trafficked is Hollywood Forever Cemetery, resting place of Dee Dee Ramone, as well as the locale of a memo-rial statue of Dee Dee's band mate Johnny Ramone, that the cemetery charges five dollars for its map.

That's just the tip of the iceberg, though. The wag who noted that Elvis's dying was "a good career move" couldn't have known how right he was. Four rockers are among the leaders on *Forbes* magazine's top-earning dead celebrities list: Elvis (number one), John Lennon (number four), George Harrison (number seven), and Bob Marley (number nine). In 2004, that quartet racked up more than seventy-five million dollars in music and merchandise sales.

For planning your own grave-visiting expeditions, author Scott Stanton's guide *Tombstone Tourist: Musicians,* among other volumes, offers directions to the resting places of numerous rockers. Online, there are several sites devoted to the subject. The most complete and accurate is findagrave.com, which catalogues thousands of celebrity resting places, as well as those of seven million other folks who are less exalted.

Findagrave is an interactive site: Anyone can send in pictures and directions to grave sites, some of which are remarkably detailed. R&B singer Aaliyah, for instance, is buried in the Ferncliff Cemetery and Mausoleum in Hartsdale, New York, Unit M-11, BBB, C-114. And Tex-Mex master Doug Sahm ("She's About a Mover") lies in San Antonio, Texas' Sunset Memorial Park at GPS coordinates: 29.29953, -98.25939.

Whatever the reason for visiting the resting places of our heroes, part of it has to do with our love of the music itself. Our presence at these cemeteries and mausoleums announces that there is an unbroken chain that stretches back to the roots of the form; and by extension, links to the future. As it says on the headstone of Blues Brother John Belushi, I MAY BE GONE, BUT ROCK AND ROLL LIVES ON.

— *J.D. Reed*

FOLLOWING PAGES: *Mementos at the tombstones of punk guitarist Johnny Thunders and original Beatle Stu Sutcliffe*

An eclectic collection left for punk rocker Dee Dee Ramone

BUDDY HOLLY
September 7, 1936–February 3, 1959

J.P. "THE BIG BOPPER" RICHARDSON
October 24, 1930–February 3, 1959

RITCHIE VALENS
May 13, 1941–February 3, 1959

OPPOSITE PAGE: *Part of this crash-site sculpture now hangs in an Iowa tavern.*

The Day the Music Died

*F*ebruary 3, 1959: "The day the music died." So it is immortalized in Don McLean's "American Pie," and so it was on that snowy night in Clear Lake, Iowa. Headliner Buddy Holly, going it alone without the Crickets, seventeen-year-old Latino rising star Ritchie Valens, and DJ turned singer J.P. "the Big Bopper" Richardson, of "Chantilly Lace" fame, were in the middle of a badly organized Midwest tour called the Winter Dance Party. Their buses were dilapidated and so poorly heated that some musicians became ill.

After their Surf Ballroom gig in Clear Lake, Holly boarded a Beechcraft Bonanza he had hired to fly him and his sidemen to their next stop, Fargo, North Dakota. He hoped they could rest and even get their laundry done once there. At the last minute, though, his bassist (and future country star), Waylon Jennings, graciously gave up his seat to Richardson, who was suffering with the flu. And Holly's guitarist Tommy Allsup lost his place to Valens in a coin flip. The single-engine craft lifted off at 2:00 a.m. and crashed into a frozen cornfield a few minutes later, killing the three musicians and the pilot.

They were buried in their hometowns beneath modest markers: Texans Holly (originally Holley) in Lubbock, and Richardson in Beaumont. Valens was interred in California's San Fernando Valley. But twenty years later, Clear Lake finally acknowledged that it was home to a transforming American catastrophe. In 1979, the town commemorated the event with a "Winter Dance Party" memorial concert, which has been repeated every year since. The

Holly rests in his hometown, Lubbock, Texas, under his birth name.

Valens's mother outlived her son by almost thirty years; they are buried in Los Angeles near the grave of William Frawley (I Love Lucy's Fred Mertz).

February show, now held in the restored high kitsch of the Surf Ballroom, has attracted acts from the late Del Shannon to Hootie and the Blowfish to Faith Hill.

In 1988, Wisconsin sculptor Ken Paquette made the pilgrimage to the crash site. "I was surprised that there was no kind of marker," he said. He soon made a burnished-aluminum construction, representing a guitar and three LP-like discs, each bearing a name. A few years ago, the sculpture was vandalized. The discs were stolen and the guitar badly twisted. Paquette replaced the sculpture with a duplicate, and the old guitar piece was auctioned on eBay, bringing three thousand dollars to benefit a music scholarship. Its new Clear Lake home: above the bar at Elly's Lakefront Tap.

Nearly a half-century on, the echoes of that last Holly concert whisper across the frozen corn stubble – and through the spirit of the music. It has become a tradition that if you appear at the Surf, you sign the wall of the small dressing room. And when she visited some years back, Holly's widow, Maria Elena, spoke for everyone when she scribbled in black marker, RAVE ON! ✄

OPPOSITE PAGE AND ABOVE: *The Big Bopper's marker in Beaumont, Texas, features musical details.*

ϛene vincent
February 11, 1935–October 12, 1971

*O*nce asked what was the smartest thing ever said in rock & roll, Paul Simon replied without missing a beat: "Be-Bop-a-Lula, she's my baby." All grease, leather, crooked teeth, and raw recklessness, Gene Vincent was the alternative Elvis, the one who remained true to his rockabilly roots. A blitzkrieg drinker and womanizer (he married and divorced four times), he charted in the mid-fifties and toured relentlessly. When American pop demanded more clean-cut acts, the Virginia native subsisted on his considerable European fan base.

Vincent was plagued by a painful deformation of his leg due to a motorcycle accident, and the limb was further damaged in 1960, when a car he was riding in with fellow rockabilly star Eddie Cochran crashed near London. Cochran was killed. While convalescing, Vincent played the U.K. pub circuit, but his career never picked up again. Suffering from leg pain and bleeding ulcers, he moved back to the States in September 1971. On October 12, critically ill and weak, the thirty-six-year-old Vincent was picked up by his parents, Kie and Louise Craddock, and driven to their home in Saugus, California. As he entered their modest house trailer, he tripped and fell and was taken to nearby Inter-Valley Community Hospital. There, he died of "acute hepatic insufficiency due to, or as a consequence of, cirrhosis of the liver."

His humble funeral was conducted by controversial Tennessee evangelists Tony and Susan Alamo (later imprisoned for income tax evasion), whom Gene's mother had been following. The Alamos even paid for the singer's plot at Eternal Valley Memorial Park, in Newhall, California. But his grave remained bare until 1976, when his last wife, Jackie Frisco, had a headstone made featuring the musical notation for the chorus of "Be-Bop-a-Lula." But, "The sad part of it is," said rocker and Vincent fan Marshall Crenshaw, "they have it written incorrectly." ✄

The grave of the rockabilly pioneer went unmarked for five years.

eddie cochran

October 3, 1938–April 17, 1960

Cochran was killed in a U.K. car crash that also injured Vincent.

The spring of 1960 was to be Eddie Cochran's moment to grab the brass ring. The twenty-one-year-old California-born guitarist, who penned and performed the teen-discontent anthem "Summertime Blues," was wowing British crowds with over-the-top performances. A young George Harrison followed him from town to town, and T. Rex front-man Marc Bolan later bragged that he once carried Cochran's orange Gretsch to a waiting limo. Cochran's U.K. tour was so successful that it was extended from five to fifteen weeks, and Cochran decided to fly home for a break for a few days. After a show at the Hippodrome Theatre in Bristol, he shared a taxi to Heathrow Airport with his song-writer girlfriend Sharon Sheeley, who wrote the Rick Nelson hit "Poor Little Fool," and his touring pal Gene Vincent. The cab blew a tire in the village of Chippenham, Wiltshire, swerved out of control, and crashed into a lamppost. The driver was badly injured, Vincent suffered a broken collarbone and a leg injury, and Sheeley's pelvis was broken. Cochran was thrown through the windshield. He was rushed to St. Martin's Hospital in Bath but died of head injuries later that day. He was the first rock & roll star to die on U.K. soil, and in one of those eerie convergences that seem to pepper the music's legacy, a few days after his death, his latest single was released: "Three Steps to Heaven."

Cochran was buried quietly near his California home in Forest Lawn Memorial Park in Cypress, under a wordy bronze slab. A memorial stone at the crash site in Wiltshire still draws fans each year on the singer's birthday.

ROBERT JOHNSON
May 8, 1911–August 16, 1938

RIGHT: *This etching on the centograph of Johnson's Morgan City grave site replaces a sketch of the bluesman by cartoonist R. Crumb, which was twice stolen.*

OPPOSITE PAGE, TOP: *This simple stone in Quito, Mississippi, is thought to mark the least likely place in which Johnson rests.*

BORN IN HAZLEHURST, COPIAH COUNTY, THE RECORDING CAREER AND BRIEF TRANSIT OF ROBERT JOHNSON LEFT AN ENORMOUS LEGACY TO AMERICAN MUSIC, PRESERVED FOR THE AGES BY THE COLUMBIA RECORDING COMPANY. THE BODY OF HIS WORK IS CONSIDERED TO BE AMONG THE MOST POWERFUL OF ITS KIND, A HAUNTING AND LYRICAL PORTRAIT OF THE HUMAN SPIRIT.

ROBERT JOHNSON
"KING OF THE DELTA BLUES SINGERS"
HIS MUSIC STRUCK A CHORD THAT CONTINUES TO RESONATE. HIS BLUES ADDRESSED GENERATIONS HE WOULD NEVER KNOW AND MADE POETRY OF HIS VISIONS AND FEARS.

Robert Johnson went out like a rocker. The Delta bluesman was served poisoned whiskey by a jealous husband in a Mississippi juke joint. Johnson was only twenty-seven and had recorded just twenty-nine songs when he died. But his style and his tunes – including "I Believe I'll Dust My Broom" and "Sweet Home Chicago" – were destined to become the backbone of black urban music. Little enough is known about the guitarist: He wandered the South, playing for change in roadhouses and bars. He famously claimed that one night at a country crossroads, he sold his soul to the devil for the talent in his fingers.

Like his life, Johnson's final resting place is a matter of mystery: It may be in one of three Mississippi cemeteries, though for five decades none of the sites bore a marker. His death certificate indicates, however, that he was buried at Mount Zion Church near Morgan City, and in 1988, Skip Henderson, a New Jersey guitar dealer and blues aficionado, began an effort to erect a Johnson memorial there. When he found that the small black church was deeply in debt, Henderson persuaded Columbia Records, which issued Johnson's music, to pony up ten thousand dollars to pay off the church mortgage and donate more money to buy a monument. "I designed a cenotaph on a napkin at the bar of the Peabody Hotel in Memphis," Henderson recalled. "Peter Guralnick [author of *Searching for Robert Johnson*] wrote the words, and the cartoonist R. Crumb did a sketch of Johnson, which I had engraved on an enamel medallion." The only problem? "One side of the cenotaph lists all of Johnson's songs, like 'Hellhound on My Trail' and 'Drunken Hearted Man.' The church elders didn't want that toward their entrance, so it faces the highway."

The medallion by Crumb was stolen twice and eventually replaced with a likeness of Johnson etched into the stone.

A second marker is at Payne's Chapel in tiny Quito, only a few miles from Mount Zion. Richard Johnson, a deacon, claimed to be a descendent of Robert's and believed that he was buried there. In 1991, a local woman known only as Queen Elizabeth gave a disjointed account of Johnson's burial at the chapel. Inspired by the story, an Atlanta bar band, appropriately called the Tombstones, bought a stone marker. The flat stone bears the odd inscription, RESTING IN THE BLUES.

The third, and some say most likely spot, is Little Zion M.B. Church, in Greenwood, the self-styled Cotton Capital of the World. Elderly resident Rosie Eskridge recalled that her husband Tom had

dug Johnson's grave. She took him a glass of water when he'd finished, and she saw him put up a little wooden marker: ROBERT JOHNSON. In 2001, record producer Stephen LaVere, a onetime agent for Johnson's estate, had another marker installed in the cemetery.

Which grave contains Robert Johnson? His remains may not be in any of them. But that doesn't deter fans following the blues highway through the endless cotton fields: All three markers are decorated by beer bottle tops, notes, guitar picks, and potted plants. In the long run, it doesn't matter which stone he is under, if any. In fact, the ambiguity makes Johnson's poetry that much more powerful. "You may bury my body down by highway side," he sang. "So my own evil spirit can catch a Greyhound bus and ride." ✄

Both sides of this marker at Greenwood's Little Zion M.B. Church carry words by Johnson, including handwritten lyrics penned shortly before his death.

Hank Williams
September 17, 1923–January 1, 1953

A marble Stetson honors Williams's "Luke the Drifter" gospel-singer persona.

Twenty-four years before Elvis's death, Hank Williams set the mark for how an American icon checks out: dramatically, drugged, and before his time. Like Presley, the Hillbilly Shakespeare was falling from a stellar orbit, one that forever changed country music. His plainspoken, bluesy anthems like "Your Cheatin' Heart," "Hey, Good Lookin', " and "I'm So Lonesome I Could Cry" would infuse rock & roll with their confessional intensity. But by age twenty-eight, Williams was so debilitated from abuse of alcohol and painkillers that he was fired from the Grand Ole Opry for frequent no-shows, was acrimoniously divorced from his first wife, and, while wedding a second time, conceived a child out of wedlock with a third woman.

Because of bad weather, the singer/songwriter couldn't fly from Knoxville, Tennessee, to a date in Canton, Ohio. On New Year's Eve, 1952, he set out for the show in a rented a Cadillac with a teenage chauffer to drive him. At the Andrew Johnson Hotel before leaving, the singer was injected with vitamin B12 and morphine by a doctor for his bad back. He climbed into the backseat with a bottle of whiskey and died somewhere on the road.

His funeral drew more than twenty thousand people to the Montgomery Auditorium, the largest crowd in the Alabama city since Jefferson Davis was inaugurated president of the Confederacy. Ex-wife Audrey (mother of Hank Jr.), then-wife Billie Jean (who would later marry singer Johnny Horton), and girlfriend Bobbie Jett (who gave birth to daughter Jett Williams five days after the funeral) were among the mourners who heard Roy Acuff, Red Foley, and Ernest Tubb offer Williams's enduring gospel turn "I Saw the Light."

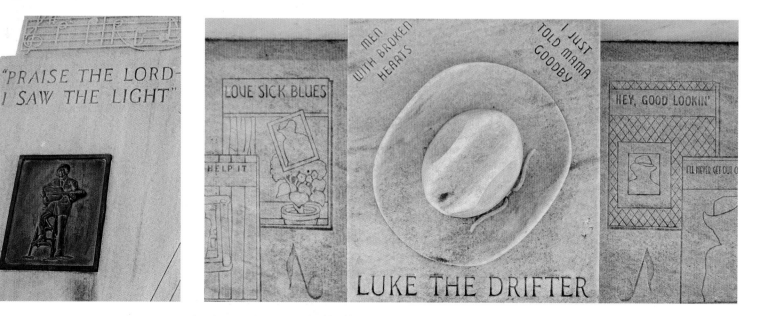

Williams's elaborate grave, in Montgomery's Oakwood Annex Cemetery, remains a beacon of idol worship. Though, like Elvis's, this final resting place is Williams's second. For two weeks after he died, his remains rested in a less propitious spot. Pressured by the family, the cemetery consolidated the plots of several French pilots killed while training at a nearby air base during World War II. That opened the area at the top of a rise where Williams now resides; Audrey was later buried alongside him. Foot traffic is so heavy that the area in front of the markers had to be covered in Astroturf. Visitors leave guitar picks, notes, whiskey bottles, and money on the marble brim of Williams's signature hat. The charged atmosphere led singer Alan Jackson to pen a song about visiting the grave: "Midnight in Montgomery/He's always singing there." ✄

Williams's spectacular grave, with its country filagree, draws so many tourists that the grass was replaced with artificial turf.

Duane Allman
November 20, 1946–October 29, 1971

Berry Oakley
April 4, 1948–November 11, 1972

The Allman Brothers

There couldn't be a more fitting resting place for Duane Allman and Berry Oakley than Macon, Georgia's Rose Hill Cemetery. The band mates, who died in motorcycle accidents within one year of each other, and just two blocks apart, are buried here side by side. The 165-year-old graveyard with its Italianate terraces, where some 600 Confederate dead are interred, was a favorite hangout for the fledgling Allman Brothers Band in the mid-sixties. The rebels who revolutionized Southern rock used Rose Hill as a backdrop on their first album cover, and one of their songs, "In Memory of Elizabeth Reed," garnered its title from the headstone of long-time Rose Hill resident Elizabeth Napier Reed.

But far from serenity at the jasmine-scented cemetery, the rockers' graves have roiled local waters and frayed family members' nerves. By some reckoning, they are Macon's top tourist draw, featured on the city's Web site and listed in chamber of commerce brochures. More than a thousand pilgrims from around the world visit the graves each month, and the morning detritus attests to hard partying: empty whiskey bottles, marijuana roaches, panties, condoms. Fans used to carve their initials into the soft Georgia marble of the slabs, spray-paint graffiti on them, and chip off pieces as souvenirs. An attempt was even made to dig up Duane's grave.

That was more than enough for Berry Oakley's younger sister, Candace, and her husband Buford Birdsey. "The city won't provide any security," she said, "so we hire guards at times, and we try to patrol the graves ourselves." In 1998, Oakley, the only Allman Brothers relative living in Macon, surrounded the graves with chain-link fence topped with razor wire. The city, which owns the cemetery, soon removed it. Said then-mayor Jim Marshall, "It's entirely legitimate for her to want to protect her brother's grave, but this is not the way."

Some members of the Georgia Allman Brothers Band Association, a nonprofit fan club that helps clean up the grave sites, agree. "Candace needs to lighten up," said one fan. "It's the Allmans' spirit and essence that brings people. What does she think *they* did down at Rose Hill?" Oakley remains on guard. "I don't get it. The fans leave empty beer cans. If they're expecting Duane and Berry to get up at night and enjoy their 'tributes,' why don't they leave a full beer?" ✂

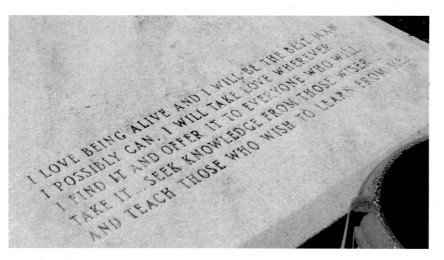

Lines from Allman's writings adorn his slab.

OPPOSITE PAGE: *The graves of Allman and Oakley are one of Macon, Georgia's top tourist draws.*

STU SUTCLIFFE
June 23, 1940–April 10, 1962

BRIAN JONES
February 28, 1942–July 3, 1969

A Beatle and a Stone

Death draws eerie parallels. Stu Sutcliffe and Brian Jones were founding members of Britain's greatest groups: Sutcliffe was an original Beatle; Jones was lead guitarist of the Rolling Stones. Yet both men, dead in their twenties, have receded in memory behind the juggernauts of the bands they helped to form.

Sutcliffe was inept on bass guitar but had a gift for style. He suggested the name Beetles (morphed to Beatles) as a take on Buddy Holly's Crickets, and his long shag-cut do became a Beatles signature. However, he left the group in 1961 to devote himself to his art and to live in Germany with photographer-girlfriend Astrid Kirchherr. For some time, he had suffered blinding headaches and irrational mood swings. On April 10, he died of a cerebral hemorrhage on the way to a Hamburg hospital. Sutcliffe's body was returned to his hometown of Huyton, England, where he was buried in Parish Church Cemetery. As a tribute, the Beatles put a picture of him on the cover of their 1967 album, *Sgt. Pepper's Lonely Hearts Club Band.*

Unlike Sutcliffe, Brian Jones was an accomplished guitarist who played and lived like the devil. He convinced pals Mick Jagger and Keith Richards to join the group he named after a Muddy Waters tune. But by 1969, Jones was a drug-addled wreck, barely able to make studio sessions, and Jagger and Richards asked him to leave the group. Less than a month later, he was found floating in the swimming pool of Cotchford Farm, his country estate south of London and the former home of A.A. Milne, creator of *Winnie the Pooh.* No witnesses came

Stu Sutcliffe shares a plot with his father in Huyton, England.

forward at the coroner's inquest, and, although traces of alcohol and drugs were found in his system, his drowning was ruled "death by misadventure." The conclusion has fueled decades of rumors that Jones was murdered. One plausible but unsubstantiated scenario was advanced by Jones's girlfriend Anna Wohlin. She claimed Jones fell out with building contractor Frank Thorogood about shoddy workmanship on his home. An angry Thorogood, she believed, drowned the rocker. On his deathbed, in 1993, Thorogood purportedly confessed to killing Jones, but charges were never filed, nor was the case reopened.

Bassist Bill Wyman and drummer Charlie Watts were among the mourners elbowing through thousands of onlookers outside Priory Road Cemetery in Jones's hometown of Prestbury for the graveside ceremony. Two days after Jones's death, at an afternoon gig in London's Hyde Park in broiling weather, Jagger read from Shelley's poem "Adonais": "Peace, peace! he is not dead, he doth not sleep/ He hath awakened from the dream of life." Then two thousand white butterflies were released in Jones's memory. They were meant to rise up in an inspirational cloud. But many had died in the oppressive humidity, and the rest flew only briefly and fell lifeless into the crowd. ✄

Murder or accident? The drowning death of the Rolling Stone guitarist remains a mystery.

JIMI HENDRIX
November 27, 1942–September 18, 1970

Eric Burdon refused to attend the funeral. The former lead singer of the Animals insisted that his friend Jimi Hendrix hated his hometown and would be appalled to spend eternity in Seattle.

Still, headliners gathered for the open-casket service at the Dunlop Baptist Church for the man whose playing transformed rock & roll. Thirteen days after Hendrix died in London from inhaling vomit after taking barbiturates, two hundred family, friends, and former sidemen congregated. Miles Davis, who had planned to do an album with Hendrix, showed up along with bluesman Johnny Winter and drummer Buddy Miles. But the Emerald City wasn't quite ready for center stage. When Rev. Harold Blackburn intoned, "We have to remember the great guitar player in the sky," Hendrix manager Bob Levine recalled to biographer John McDer-

mott, "We all broke up laughing. It helped ease the tension." But grieving girlfriend Devon Wilson, immortalized in Hendrix's "Dolly Dagger," found no relief. As his casket was lowered at Greenwood Memorial Park and Cemetery in suburban Renton, Washington, she tried to jump into the open grave. (In 1991, another former Hendrix girlfriend, Kathy Etchingham, prodded Scotland Yard into reopening the investigation of Hendrix's death. No new evidence was found.)

The guitarist, who issued only four albums during his lifetime, left behind a tangle of deals and contracts and a ton of unpublished music. Some one hundred records of widely varying quality were released by various companies after his death, but the opportunism came to an end in 1995. Jimi's father, Al Hendrix, aided by Microsoft billionaire

OPPOSITE PAGE, RIGHT: *In 2002, Hendrix's headstone and casket were moved to a soaring, handicapped-accessible memorial, where his remains share space with those of his father and other relatives.*

OPPOSITE PAGE, LEFT: *Hendrix's signature decorates the granite.*

The guitarist's original grave

and Hendrix überfan Paul Allen, gained the rights to all of his son's work. But since Al's 2002 death and his appointment of Jimi's stepsister Janie Hendrix to oversee the guitarist's $30 million estate, the family has squabbled. As late as 2004, Jimi's brother Leon, who had been cut out of the will, appealed for a percentage on the grounds that he was "the bloodline." The judge denied his suit, ruling that "Janie was the family member Al trusted most."

The power of the Hendrix mystique has never waned. In 2000, Allen opened Seattle's $240 million Experience Music Project, named after the Hendrix tune "Are You Experienced?" and built around his own collection of Hendrix memorabilia.

Hendrix's grave, at first marked with a simple ground-level headstone, was moved in 2002 to a circular memorial that features a dome supported by granite columns. Al Hendrix and his wife Ayako "June" Hendrix (Jimi's stepmother) now rest there in burial vaults at the center of the memorial. Some fifteen thousand visitors trek to the musician's grave in out-of-the-way Renton each year. They leave behind flowers, notes, guitar picks, and occasionally drug paraphernalia. Hendrix himself presaged such homage with wry wit. "It's funny the way most people love death," he once said. "Once you are dead, you are made for life . . ." ❧

JIM MORRISON
December 8, 1943–July 3, 1971

Nobody could play dead like Jim Morrison. At parties, during recording sessions, and onstage, the performer of Dionysian anthems including "Light My Fire" and "The End" would without warning collapse in a heap and lie as still as the grave, scaring the bejesus out of everyone. Perhaps that is why his grave has remained for almost thirty-five years one of the top five tourist attractions in Paris. "We have one and a half million visitors a year," said a spokesman for venerable Père-Lachaise cemetery in the City of Light, where Morrison is buried. "For the most part, they come and see Jim."

No one now can say for sure, notes biographer Stephen Davis, how the Lizard King met eternity. But this much seems certain: The twenty-seven-year-old's longtime lover Pamela Courson found him lifeless in the bathtub of their Paris apartment in the early hours of July 3, 1971, after a night of boozing and snorting heroin. She called Alain Ronay, a pal who had gone to UCLA with Morrison. Ronay realized the death had to be kept quiet. The demise of rock's preeminent demigod would set off a global media firestorm, to say nothing of a criminal investigation if drug involvement was suspected.

Ronay told the police that the deceased was Douglas (his middle name) Morrison. The authorities, however, would not let the body be moved to a funeral home while they dawdled over the paperwork of a foreigner's death. It stayed in the apartment until July 6, and a mortuary worker brought dry ice twice a day. The eventual certificate listed the cause of death as heart failure. Morrison was quickly dressed in an ill-fitting dark suit, placed in a cheap wooden coffin, and the top was hastily screwed on.

The psychedelic shaman of the sixties was laid to rest in a crowded corner of the vast, two-hundred-year-old Père-Lachaise, where Chopin, Edith Piaf, Isadora Duncan, Oscar Wilde, and dozens of other renowned artists are interred. While alive, the Doors frontman had enjoyed wandering through the baroque graveyard, strangely energized by its spooky vibe. He said he wanted to be buried there. There were few plots available, however, but when Ronay explained that Jim was an American poet, a place was found.

The graveside ceremony was meager. Pamela, Ronay, Morrison's secretary, filmmaker friend Agnes Varda, and Doors manager Bill Siddons bowed their heads and threw dirt on the coffin. A French woman named Madame Colinette tending a grave nearby found the observances disgraceful. "Everything was done in a hurry," she later told a German fanzine editor. "No priest was present, everybody left quickly. The whole scene was piteous and miserable."

Many refused to believe that the sexual anarchist who tried to set the night on fire died in such mundane circumstances. Some insisted that he had dramatically OD'd days before in Rock and Roll Circus, a notorious club. Others theorized that he had faked his own death so he could disappear, evading the pitfalls of superstardom and morphing into the filmmaker/poet he yearned to be. Doors keyboardist Ray Manzarek threw gasoline on the speculation, saying in 1974, "He could just be off and wandering around somewhere."

Morrison's grave became a pop-culture rune stone. Legions of tourists trooped by as if the patch of bare dirt was another must-see masterpiece in the Louvre. And every day, an international cadre of

fans from tie-dyed graybeards to over-pierced grungers hung out playing Doors music, smoking joints, and drinking prodigiously. They spray-painted epigraphs and obscenities on nearby tomb-stones and crypts. They left beer cans, cheap lighters, whiskey bottles, hash pipes, pills, and syringes as offerings on the grave.

The scandalous behavior shocked and angered the French, and escalating troubles marred the quiet of Père-Lachaise. At one point, riot police used tear gas on an unruly crowd of worshipers. Then two people were nabbed trying to dig up Morrison's coffin. Morrison's estate finally had a cube of gran-ite placed over the grave. It bears a Greek inscrip-tion, KATA TON DAIMONA ("True to his own spirit"). But that seemed only to increase problems. On the twentieth anniversary of his death, thou-sands rioted at the grave. After they were expelled, they continued demonstrating on the street, late at night, chanting and setting cars on fire. Security

guards (paid for by the estate), closed-circuit cam-eras, and nighttime floodlights now protect the singer's resting place. In 2001, the thirtieth anniver-sary of Morrison's death was more orderly. "It is important not to get too excited," said Thierry Bouvier, the cemetery's director. "We aren't going to kick out the ones who are just dead drunk."

The lease on Morrison's plot was set to expire in 2001, none too soon for many Parisians, who wanted his remains shipped back to America. But the estate arranged and paid for a perpetual lease, and the government, realizing that this troublesome creature was now part of the Gallic landscape, pronounced that M. Morrison was welcome to stay in France.

Time rocks on, but Jim Morrison's magnetism attracts each new generation. The Doors made only seven albums, but by the end of the twentieth century, they had sold a breathtaking fifty million records. One fan seemed to understand the enig-matic appeal when he scrawled on a nearby marker, "This is not the End." ✁

LEFT AND TOP RIGHT: *The bust of the Lizard King adorning his Paris plot was vandalized before being stolen.*

RIGHT: *Morrison's family bought this cube-shaped stone after a foiled 1986 attempt to dig up his body.*

FOLLOWING PAGES: *An international tribe of Morrison worshipers converged on Père-Lachaise in the spring of 1992.*

Gram Parsons
November 5, 1946–September 19, 1973

The saga of pioneering country rocker Gram Parsons's body began with a pact made at a funeral. Appalled at the staid religious ceremony for Byrds guitarist Clarence White, killed by a drunk driver, Parsons and his pal Phil "the Mangler" Kaufman, rock & roll's famously unhinged road manager, agreed that when one of them died the other would make sure his ashes were scattered at Joshua Tree National Monument in California's Mojave Desert.

Two months later, the singer/songwriter, who emulated the substance intake of his friend Keith Richards but didn't have the metabolism for it, was two days into a round-the-clock party with pals at his favorite retreat, the Joshua Tree Inn. Late at night on September 18, he was found unconscious in Room 8. Panicked buddies tried to revive him, but he died of what his autopsy revealed to be "drug toxicity, days, due to multiple drug use, weeks."

The singer's stepfather, Bob Parsons, claimed the body, reportedly in hopes that Louisiana law would entitle him to part of the musician's estate. (It didn't.) While the casket awaited a cargo flight to New Orleans, Kaufman set out to honor his pledge. He borrowed a hearse belonging to eccentric heiress Dale McElroy, roped in her boyfriend Michael Martin, loaded up a five-gallon gas can, and sped to Los Angeles International Airport. The well-oiled pair convinced authorities that they were empowered to take Parsons's body to another airport for transport on a private aircraft.

LEFT AND OPPOSITE PAGE: *The singer's body was stolen and cremated at Joshua Tree near Cap Rock.*

TOP RIGHT: *Parsons was finally buried outside New Orleans.*

At Joshua Tree, they stopped the hearse near a formation called Cap Rock and dropped the casket on the ground. They uncovered the body, poured on the fuel, and lit it. The result was a stunning fireball. By the time the flames burned out, the duo had fled the scene. They were eventually arrested and fined for theft of a coffin. The judge also sentenced them to a year's probation. Parsons's remains were finally flown to New Orleans for burial.

The legend around Parsons's last ride gave him a renown that eluded him in life. At a number of tribute concerts and on several recordings, his songs have been covered by such artists as Emmylou Harris, Beck, Sheryl Crow, and Elvis Costello. Fans still make the trek to Cap Rock, frequently spending the night in Room 8 at the Joshua Tree Inn. Some find their way to Parsons's modest marker in the Garden of Memories Cemetery off Airline Highway outside New Orleans. The grave site will be enhanced by a bronze likeness of Parsons by sculptor Thomas Bruno sometime in 2005. ✂

JIM CROCE
January 10, 1943–September 20, 1973

The "Time in a Bottle" singer's grave near Valley Forge is seldom visited.

There never seems to be enough time/To do the things you want to do," sang Jim Croce. The sentiment proved all too true for the Philadelphia-raised singer/songwriter: He died at age thirty. While flying to a Texas gig, his private craft hit a pecan tree and crashed in Natchitoches, Louisiana, killing all five people onboard. It was the day after Gram Parsons died of a drug overdose in the Mojave Desert.

Croce's grave marker in the Hyam Solomon Cemetery of Frazer, Pennsylvania, not far from Valley Forge, is unassuming. "It's not like it ever became a big shrine to Jim or anything," said his widow, Ingrid Croce. "That would have been offensive to him. It's a quiet spot, under a pine tree. Jim loved pine trees, and he was an avid historian, so we felt the Valley Forge area was the perfect place."

Croce, like many performers who die young and violently before their fame has jelled, found his audience beyond the hush of the cemetery. His ageless hit "Time in a Bottle" shot to Number One within months of his death, and three of his posthumous albums have made the Top Twenty. A decade after his death, as a tribute to her late husband, Ingrid opened Croce's Restaurant and Jazz Bar in San Diego, where their musician son, A.J. Croce, sometimes performs. In 1996, Ingrid published a memory-filled cookbook, *Thyme in a Bottle*. ✄

HARRY CHAPIN
December 7, 1942–July 16, 1981

Long Island–based singer/songwriter Harry Chapin was a baby-boom folk rocker who gained notice for his heartfelt 1970s story-songs: "Taxi" and "Cat's in the Cradle." But he made a larger impact as a dedicated social activist. He donated more than five million dollars to charity, cofounded the nonprofit group World Hunger Year (WHY), and lobbied Congress on a number of issues. On his fatal day, the troubadour was speeding west along New York's Long Island Expressway in his blue Volkswagen Rabbit. He was a dreadful driver who had collected so many tickets that his license had been revoked months earlier. Near Exit 40, Chapin had turned on his emergency blinkers and was changing lanes toward the shoulder when he was hit from behind by a tractor-trailer. The VW skidded and caught fire; the truck driver and

another motorist managed to drag Chapin from the burning wreckage. But the thirty-eight-year-old died of a massive heart attack, a spokesman at Nassau County Medical Center said. It could not be determined, however, if he was stricken before or after the collision. He was slated to play a free concert in East Meadow that night. Told of Chapin's death, the grieving crowd lit candles and sang his usual set ender, "Circle."

Chapin's wife, Sandy, the couple's five children, and close friends attended the low-key graveside service at the Huntington Rural Cemetery, near Chapin's home. "From here . . . you can see all of Huntington without any sign of different neighborhoods," said Sandy, standing by the oak casket. "Harry always wanted to break down barriers between different sections and regions." Chapin's marker, a boulder from his family's farm in Andover, New Jersey, bearing lyrics from his song "I Wonder What Would Happen to This World," is still adorned by fans with messages painted on stones. Said friend Bill Ayres, who cofounded WHY and appreciated the musician's spiritual side, "Harry once said to me that if there is a God, it must be a God who recognizes our weaknesses and then hugs us. Well, now Harry knows who God is. He beat us on that one, too." ✂

Chapin's boulder headstone is sometimes decorated with hand-painted stones.

RANDY RHOADS
December 6, 1956–March 19, 1982

From Buddy Holly to Otis Redding to Jim Croce, no airplane fatality is more of a freak accident than that of heavy-metal guitar god Randy Rhoads. In 1979, the former Quiet Riot guitarist became a member of Ozzy Osbourne's band, with whom he was touring three years later in Florida. On March 19, 1982, Ozzy's bus driver Andrew Aycock, whose pilot's license wasn't valid, was at the controls of a borrowed Model 35 Beechcraft Bonanza, buzzing the group's tour bus for a lark. Onboard the plane were Rhoads and the band's hairdresser/makeup artist Rachel Youngblood, while the rest of the company was on the bus. On the third pass, a wing tip hit the vehicle.

The plane was thrown sideways, clipped a pine tree, and crashed into flames when it collided with the garage of a Leesburg mansion on a private airfield called Flying Baron Estates. No one on the ground was injured, but all three in the Beechcraft were killed. Rhoads was twenty-five.

Ozzy's band and Quiet Riot members were among those attending Rhoads's funeral in San Bernardino, California. Music teacher Arlene Thomas, a close friend, sang and played acoustic guitar before Rhoads was interred in Mountain View Cemetery. Two years later, his body was moved to an elaborate mausoleum. "I had a small bronze guitar and the RR signature that he used put on the gravestone," said his mother, Delores Rhoads, who owns a North Hollywood music school. "I know he would have wanted that."

Rhoads's reputation never waned. In the late nineties, the Jackson guitar company, which still markets a $3,000 Randy Rhoads Flying V style guitar, issued a limited edition of a Randy Rhoads "high-end collectible" action figure. And in 2003, Sharon Osbourne, riding the wave of her eccentric family's reality TV series, revealed another kind of action. In her tell-all, *Ordinary People: Our Story,* she admitted that she slept with the guitarist on tour, before she married Ozzy, in late 1982. In 2004, a bronze bust of Rhoads was installed on Hollywood's Rockwalk. Said Ozzy at the ceremony, "He was a small guy with a giant talent. Not a day goes by that my family doesn't think about him." ✖

Killed in a bizarre plane crash, the Ozzy Osbourne guitarist was laid to rest in a vault that sports elaborate details as well as lipstick kisses.

NICK DRAKE
June 18, 1948–November 25, 1974

RIGHT: *Drake is buried with his parents in rural England.*

OPPOSITE PAGE: *Some of Drake's lyrics grace one side of his headstone.*

FOLLOWING PAGES: *His fans, many of whom were children when he died, leave poignant talismans at his bucolic resting place.*

"Now we rise, and we are everywhere." The lyric from the last song on Nick Drake's final album, *Pink Moon*, engraved on the back of his headstone, is eerily prescient. The reclusive English singer/songwriter's three albums sold minimally during his lifetime, and he performed only a handful of times. But three decades after his apparent suicide from ingesting antidepressants (a coroner's ruling that his parents contested), his melancholy music has attracted a cadre of admirers. Groups including R.E.M., Coldplay, and Radiohead hail the Cambridge University dropout a genius, and fan Brad Pitt narrated a recent BBC radio documentary about him. Drake reached a worldwide audience in 2000 when Volkswagen used "Pink Moon" in a TV commercial, spurring sales of a posthumous boxed set of his work.

Like his sound, Drake's headstone – under a churchyard oak tree in Solihull, Warwickshire – possesses a tranquil charm that galvanizes fans. It is close to the rural village of Tanworth-in-Arden, home of his parents, Rodney and Molly Drake, who died after their son and now rest in the same plot. A weather-beaten wood sign nailed to the oak tree asks visitors to be respectful, and so they are. "Some leave little mementos and articles of interest, but no one takes anything," says Drake fan Nigel Davies, who has made two recent trips to the site. "Considering Jim Morrison's graffiti-polluted grave in Paris, it is very pleasant to see this respect."

NOW WE RISE
AND WE ARE EVERYWHERE

DUSTY SPRINGFIELD

April 16, 1939–March 2, 1999

Get things organized," Dusty Springfield told an assistant when she knew the end was near. "I want to go out with a bit of style." So she did. The quintessential sixties singer, as renowned for her beehive do and panda-esque eye makeup as for her soulful voice, succumbed to breast cancer after a five-year battle. Per her wishes, a horse-drawn hearse with glass sides, bearing her casket and a large pink-and-white flower arrangement spelling her name, proceeded through the streets of Henley-on-Thames, the Oxfordshire, England, village where she lived.

"You Don't Have to Say You Love Me," one of her chart-toppers, played over loudspeakers as she was carried into St. Mary the Virgin Church, where she was eulogized by luminaries including Elvis Costello, Nona Hendryx, and Lulu. Neil Tennant, with whom Springfield sang a top-selling duet on the Pet Shop Boys' "What Have I Done to Deserve This?," pronounced her "the very essence

RIGHT: *Springfield's ashes were scattered in Ireland, but fans regularly decorate her marker.*

OPPOSITE PAGE: *The singer's plaque in St. Mary's church-yard, near her Oxfordshire home*

of fabness." A thousand mourners stood in a downpour to watch the funeral service via a live video link.

The White Queen of Soul was mourned as well by Queen Elizabeth II, who said from Buckingham Palace that she was "saddened" by the singer's passing. The queen awarded Springfield an OBE (Order of the British Empire) just two months before her death, but the star was too ill to appear at the palace. So her friend and manager Vicki Wickham brought the medal to her hospital room in a Fortnum & Mason bag. "What would the queen think," Springfield reportedly asked, "if she knew the OBE was in a plastic takeaway bag?"

The singer made provisions for all those close to her, including her beloved cat, a California rag doll named Nicholas. She is said to have instructed that her recordings be played for Nicholas, so that he could hear her voice, and that her nightgown should be placed in his basket. His diet: imported American baby food.

London-born Springfield, whose real name was Mary Isabel Catherine Bernadette O'Brien, was cremated and her ashes scattered at a "favorite spot" in the Irish countryside. But her marker in St. Mary's churchyard, which indicates her OBE status, is in the middle of the village. There, fans leave framed photos, potted plants, and porcelain cats.

Two weeks after she died, Springfield was inducted into the Rock and Roll Hall of Fame by Elton John, who said that her fan club was the first one he belonged to as a kid. He had been touring when she passed away, and when he learned of the death at a concert in Illinois, Sir Elton, a fellow OBE, said, "Dusty, wherever you are, this one's for you, my love." And he launched into her hit "I Only Want to Be With You." ✄

eLvis presLey

January 8, 1935–August 16, 1977

This angel was moved from Elvis's original grave to Graceland.

OPPOSITE PAGE: *The grave sites of Elvis and his family at Graceland*

*E*lvis has left the building."

That resonant, wry, bittersweet announcement has been applied to all sorts of American finality. Originally, it was broadcast at the end of the King's concerts to discourage fans from hanging around, waiting for him to belt out another tune. Ironically, when Elvis Presley exited for the last time, dead of a drug-induced heart attack at forty-two, the pronouncement was not the coda, but the kick off, to rock & roll's grandest – and strangest – encore.

As news of his death spread on the afternoon of August 16, 1977, a worldwide outpouring of grief took FTD, the national network of florists, by surprise. The service recorded its biggest single day in its history, selling thousands of arrangements, from lavish floral Bibles to single roses. (It would take more than a hundred vans to transport all the flowers to the cemetery.)

In Memphis, chaos took center stage. A crowd of fifty thousand fans and curiosity-seekers, stunned and quiet, gathered from everywhere on Elvis Presley Boulevard, in front of Graceland, Elvis's estate,

A marker honors the singer's twin, Jessie Garon, who is buried in Mississippi.

and remained there for two days. The property's stone wall was "low enough to jump over," wrote *Rolling Stone's* Chet Flippo, "but no one tried." The near-silent vigil was shattered early on the morning of the funeral when a drunk driver plowed into the throng, instantly killing two nineteen-year-old girls from Louisiana.

Inside Graceland, Elvis's grief-stricken father, Vernon, allowed fans to pay their respects against the advice of friends and security men. A line more than a mile long formed in the stultifying heat. National Guardsmen and police distributed water and ice, yet hundreds fainted as temperatures soared. Four at a time, wilting mourners climbed Graceland's winding drive to file past the copper coffin in the foyer, where Elvis lay in a white suit, powder blue shirt, and white tie.

The famous arrived amid the confusion. Caroline Kennedy, daughter of the slain president, was welcomed into the house until the family learned that she was acting as a reporter. She was politely told to leave. James Brown asked for, and was granted, a few minutes alone with Elvis. But the Godfather of Soul told the Presleys that he wouldn't attend the funeral. "I remembered Otis," he said, referring to the service for Otis Redding a decade earlier, which devolved from moving memorial into red carpet overkill.

Only a few notables, including Chet Atkins and Ann-Margret, were among the two hundred jammed into the mansion for the private service. Televangelist Rex Humbard said a few words, and gospel legend James Blackwood, one of Elvis's earliest idols, sang Presley's favorite religious song, "How Great Thou Art." Defiant of protocol to the end, Elvis's flamboyant manager, Colonel Tom Parker, leaned

✝
ELVIS
AARON
PRESLEY
JANUARY 8, 1935
AUGUST 16, 19__
SON OF
VERNON ELVIS PRESLEY
AND
GLADYS LOVE PRES___
FATHER OF
LISA MARIE PRESLEY

HE WAS A PRECIOUS GIFT FROM GOD
WE CHERISHED AND LOVED DEARLY.

HE HAD A GOD-GIVEN TALENT THAT HE SHARED
WITH THE WORLD. AND WITHOUT A DOUBT
HE BECAME MOST WIDELY ACCLAIMED;
CAPTURING THE HEARTS OF YOUNG AND OLD ALIKE.

HE WAS ADMIRED NOT ONLY AS AN ENTERTAINER,
BUT AS THE GREAT HUMANITARIAN THAT HE WAS;
FOR HIS GENEROSITY, AND HIS KIND FEELINGS
FOR HIS FELLOW MAN.

HE REVOLUTIONIZED THE FIELD OF MUSIC AND
RECEIVED ITS HIGHEST AWARDS.

HE BECAME A LIVING LEGEND IN HIS OWN TIME,
EARNING THE RESPECT AND LOVE OF MILLIONS.

GOD SAW THAT HE NEEDED SOME REST AND
CALLED HIM HOME TO BE WITH HIM.

WE MISS YOU, SON AND DADDY. I THANK GOD
THAT HE GAVE US YOU AS OUR SON.

TCB

BY VERNON PRESLEY

against a pillar in the hallway wearing his usual seersucker slacks, baseball cap, and short-sleeved shirt.

Elvis was interred in the wall of a large mausoleum at Forest Hill Cemetery, three miles north on Elvis Presley Boulevard. But eternal rest wasn't in the stars. Over the next weeks, a million or so people overwhelmed the graveyard, requiring the Presleys to employ security. There was even a badly botched scheme to steal the body. Nothing came of it, but on October 2, Vernon obtained permission from the city to move Elvis and Elvis's mother, Gladys, buried in Forest Hill since her death in 1958, to Graceland. "I guess they will finally get to rest," Vernon said.

The graves are located near a reflecting pool, in an area called the Meditation Garden, which Elvis used as a spiritual retreat. The plot later accommodated Vernon and Minne Mae Presley, Elvis's grandmother. Jessie Garon Presley, Elvis's twin brother who died at birth, is commemorated by a small plaque, although his body remains in Tupelo, Mississippi, where they were born.

During daily walk-up times to the Meditation Garden, thousands have visited Elvis's Graceland grave since he was reburied there (a local ordinance requires grave sites be accessible to the public). Elvis purists quickly complained that Elvis's middle name was misspelled on the tombstone. His parents named him Aron, perhaps to parallel Garon, Jessie's middle name. But in later life, Elvis preferred the biblical spelling Aaron, which adorns his marker.

When Graceland opened to the public in 1982, it quickly became the most famous home in America after the White House. Some seven hundred thousand visitors, who pay a minimum of eighteen dollars for the tour, stop by Elvis's grave every year. (There are still free walk-ups in the early morning

on most days.) Among those who have paid their respects are notables from Boy George to Jimmy Carter, Joan Rivers to U2, and David Copperfield to Johnny Cash. (It is not known if Michael Jackson moon-walked out to the garden when he visited Graceland in 1994 with then-wife Lisa Marie Presley.)

The grave site is continually adorned with posters, elaborate floral displays, notes, and mementos left by fans and Elvis clubs. The hundreds of teddy bears placed on the grave every year are donated to local childrens charities. But a surprising number of folks still refuse to believe that the King died. A 1988 tabloid story proclaimed that he was seen in Kalamazoo, Michigan, eating a Whopper, and Elvis sightings have become part of the American psychic landscape and the fodder of late-night monologues.

Elvis's grave remains the epicenter of an empire. Nearly three decades after his demise, thanks to Graceland tours, merchandise, and repackaged albums, Elvis pulled in forty million dollars in 2004, leading *Forbes* magazine's list of top-earning dead celebrities. In 2005, the King had his twentieth U.K. Number One hit single with the rerelease of "One Night." The same year, billionaire Robert F.X. Sillerman, who purchased a major share of the Elvis merchandising business from Lisa Marie, announced that he is considering mounting "Elvis themed" entertainment in Las Vegas, Europe, and Japan.

Although Elvis drifted far beyond rock & roll with his capes, karate poses, and patriotic medleys, the impact of his death on the music he helped create is undeniable. "We're definitely grown-ups now," said Paul Simon, who seemed to speak for a generation. "If he's dead, then we can't be kids anymore." ✄

A spooky arrangement left at Presley's grave

OPPOSITE PAGE: *A candlelight ceremony at Graceland during "Elvis Week" in 2004, twenty-seven years after the King's untimely death*

DENNIS WILSON
December 4, 1944–December 28, 1983

CARL WILSON
December 21, 1946–February 6, 1998

The Beach Boys

*T*he Beach Boys haven't done well with funerals. When their abusive taskmaster father, Murray, died in 1973, his sons Brian and Dennis Wilson, estranged from him for years, did not attend his service.

And when Dennis drowned a decade later, the family was torn by squabbles. Dennis, the unsinkable supergroup's drummer and only real surfer, was the Beach Boys' wild child. By the 1970s, Dennis was banned from touring with his brothers because of his drinking. Near the end, he was downing a fifth of vodka a day. Homeless, he stayed with friends or in cheap hotels, and at Christmastime, he was bunking on a pal's yacht, *Emerald*, moored in Marina del Rey, California. After drinking all day, he began diving into the icy water – wearing only cutoffs and a swim mask – to retrieve objects he had thrown off his own repossessed cruiser months before. When he failed to come up a final time,

observers thought it was one of his practical jokes. Rescue divers recovered his body.

A shouting match erupted at Dennis's brief funeral at Inglewood Cemetery in Los Angeles. Carl and Brian Wilson, their mother, Audree, and Dennis's three ex-wives, who attended with three of Dennis's four children, all thought he should be buried next to his father. But his third wife, Shawn Love, twenty years his junior and the daughter of his first cousin and band mate Mike Love, insisted that he be buried at sea. She prevailed: The coroner would release the body only to her. Scattering ashes into the water is one thing, but permission to drop a body in the ocean is quite another. To the rescue: President Ronald Reagan, at whose inauguration the Beach Boys had performed. He cut the local red tape.

When Carl Wilson succumbed to lung and brain cancer in 1998, it effectively ended the Beach Boys. Led by Mike Love, the group would carry on, but only as a nostalgia act; lawsuits would fly over the name and song rights, and the group's mastermind, Brian Wilson, would veer even more his own way. In the decades when Brian retreated into drug-addled mental instability, Carl had been the conduit between him and the band. He anchored live shows and in the studio sang lead on hits including "Good Vibrations" and "Kokomo." As Carl had done so many times in life, his private funeral in an L.A. church, just two months after mother Audree Wilson died, brought factions together. Brian was there, as well as Love, original guitarist Al Jardine, and Carl's wife Gina (daughter of Dean Martin). The ceremony served to purge decades of pent-up emotion. Before Carl was interred at Westwood Memorial Park, Brian Wilson broke down. Said his daughter, singer Carnie Wilson, "He really let go." ❧

Carl's brother Dennis has no grave – he was buried at sea.

JUNIOR WALKER

June 14, 1931–November 23, 1995

"Shotgun" made Junior Walker's reputation, but he was no one-hit wonder. With his raw tenor sax and gravel-rough voice fronting the All Stars, Walker racked up twenty-five singles on the *Billboard* charts, including "How Sweet It Is" and "Pucker Up, Buttercup." But Walker's star at Motown, where his unrefined sound ran counter to the label's pudding-smooth productions, dimmed with the 1970s disco craze. His influence, however, made sparks. He soloed on Foreigner's 1981 hit "Urgent," and Jerry Garcia said that the give-and-take among instruments on Walker cuts such as "Cleo's Mood" inspired the Grateful Dead's playing. Like a lot of R&B musicians from the era, Walker, born Autry De Walt Mixon, didn't see much in the way of royalties. In his last years, he lived modestly in Battle Creek, Michigan. Some hundred miles west of Detroit, "Cereal City" is the home of Kellogg and Post. Walker died of cancer in 1995 at age sixty-four, survived by nine sons and four daughters. He is buried in Battle Creek's Oak Hill Cemetery, which, like the rest of the town, perpetually smells of cooking grain. ✁

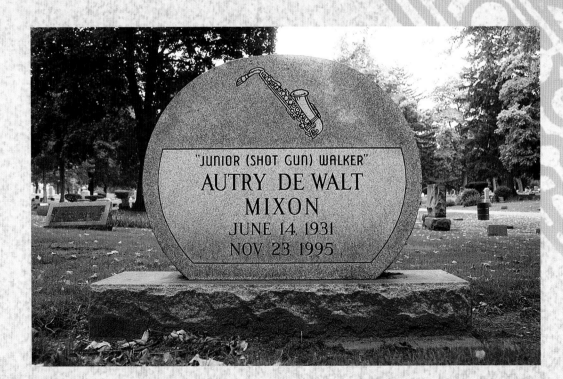

The "Shotgun" singer lies in Battle Creek, Michigan, where he spent his retirement.

minnie riperton
November 8, 1947–July 12, 1979

The R&B singer with the angelic five-octave voice keeps good company. She is interred at the Los Angeles cemetery Westwood Memorial Park, just a couple of markers from the Beach Boys' Carl Wilson, and not far from Natalie Wood and Roy Orbison. Trained in opera, Riperton veered toward pop music. She performed with various groups, singing backup for stars from Etta James to Stevie Wonder. She became indelible for one track on her 1975 solo effort, *Perfect Angel*: "Lovin' You," cowritten by Riperton and her husband and produced by Stevie Wonder. Following her death from breast cancer at age thirty-one, Jose Feliciano sang at her funeral, and Wonder was a pallbearer. "A blind pallbearer," said cemetery manager Bill Pierce, "the only time we've ever had one." Lyrics from "Lovin' You," which topped the pop and R&B charts, adorn her grave marker. "People who come to the park don't remember her until they see the lyrics," said Pierce. "Then they say, 'Oh, yes!'" Undoubtedly, many are equally unaware that Riperton was the mother of *Saturday Night Live*'s Maya Rudolph. ✀

Minnie Riperton is buried in Los Angeles.

aaliyah

January 16, 1979–August 25, 2001

*I*t is so beautiful," said fan Nicole Campbell outside Manhattan's St. Ignatius Loyola Church. "She's going out like a princess." Indeed, the cream-colored casket of Aaliyah (Swahili for "exalted one") Dana Haughton arrived in a white, horse-drawn hearse on the last leg of a royal ride. At age eleven, the singer/actress opened for her aunt Gladys Knight, in Las Vegas, and never slowed down. Aaliyah notched four platinum albums, four Number One R&B singles, a Grammy nomination, and the starring role in the movie *Queen of the Damned.*

After filming a music video on Abaco Island, the Bahamas, Aaliyah and her entourage of eight boarded a twin engine Cessna 402 B to fly to Opa-locka, Florida. Moments after takeoff from Marsh Harbour airport, the craft crashed into a hillside, killing all ten aboard. Investigators found that the plane was dangerously overloaded and that pilot Luis Blanes, who had a criminal record and was not cleared to fly the 402, showed traces of cocaine and alcohol in his blood.

Aaliyah's untimely end shocked her fans and shook the music world. The hundred or so mourners at her funeral, including Mike Tyson, Li'l Kim, Sean Combs, Usher, Jay-Z, and Gladys Knight, watched as twenty-two white doves were released, one for each year of Aaliyah's life. An all-day memorial vigil was held near Manhattan's Grand Central Station, where thousands watched a screen showing her videos. Similar events were held in Los Angeles and in Aaliyah's hometown, where there was a candlelight vigil at her alma mater, Detroit High School of Fine and Performing Arts.

The singer was interred at Ferncliff Cemetery and Mausoleum in Hartsdale, New York, where Malcolm X and Joan Crawford are buried. Visitors frequent Aaliyah's crypt, leaving flowers and pictures of the singer. Just months before she died, she seemed to prefigure her end when she described a recurring dream to an interviewer: "It's as if I am swimming in the air," she said. "Someone is following me. I don't know why. I'm scared. Then suddenly I lift off. Far away. How do I feel? Nobody can reach me. Nobody can touch me." ✼

The R&B star's funeral featured a horse-drawn hearse.

stevie ray vaughan
October 3, 1954–August 27, 1990

When first asked if Stevie Ray Vaughan had made a last-minute seating switch on the helicopter, the publicist lied. "It's just the Hollywood version," he claimed, "trying to rewrite *The Buddy Holly Story.*" The rewrite, however, was the real deal. After twenty years of one-night stands and five gold albums, the Texas guitarist, whose lightning fingers and blistering riffs were often compared to those of Jimi Hendrix, was poised for even wider acceptance. At his last gig at the Alpine Valley Music Theater near East Troy, Wisconsin, he took to the stage with the idols who had become his peers: Eric Clapton, Buddy Guy, Robert Cray, and older brother Jimmie, of the Fabulous Thunderbirds. Their last number, "Sweet Home Chicago," was a twenty-minute rave. "It was one of the most incredible sets I ever heard Stevie play," Guy said later. "I had goose bumps."

Afterward, four Bell 206 B Jet Rangers were on hand to fly the musicians back to Chicago. Originally, Vaughan was told that there were three seats available on the first chopper for himself, Jimmie, and his sister-in-law Connie Vaughan. But when he learned that only one seat was open, though three together were vacant on a later flight, he asked his brother, "Do you mind? I really need to get back." Minutes after lift off, the craft flew into a hillside, killing Vaughan, the pilot, and three members of Clapton's organization.

The loss galvanized Texas. More than five thousand fans and friends converged on an Austin park, bearing candles, messages, and boomboxes, to grieve for their homegrown star. There were two closed-casket ceremonies at Laurel Land Memorial Park in Dallas' suburban Oak Cliff. At the private rite for family and friends, Dr. John played piano as Stevie Wonder sang the Lord's Prayer. Later, more than two thousand people stood in the blazing heat for the brief public graveside service, where Bonnie Raitt, Jackson Browne, and Wonder delivered an a cappella "Amazing Grace." Stevie Ray's bronze slab, next to that of his father, Jimmie Lee, attracts thousands of visitors a year, but few leave the usual detritus of rock & roll visitations — whiskey bottles and drug paraphernalia. Vaughan, once famous for his drug and alcohol consumption, was even more renowned for being clean and sober, and proud of it, for the four years prior to his demise. ✖

Fans often leave guitar picks at Vaughan's grave.

seLena
April 16, 1971–March 31, 1995

This seal decorates the singer's Corpus Christi memorial.

Selena's grave at Seaside Memorial Park

Selena Quintanilla-Perez went from Tex-Mex idol to American legend at the Corpus Christi, Texas, Days Inn. The Grammy-winning Tejano singing sensation, poised for crossover pop stardom, had gone to the motel in her hometown to confront Yolanda Saldivar, the former president of her fan club and the manager of Selena Etc. boutique and salon, a burgeoning signature clothing business. The singer had accused Saldivar of embezzling thousands of dollars from the firm. The two argued, and as Selena stormed from a motel room, Saldivar shot her. The bullet struck the twenty-three-year-old in the back, and she staggered into the Days Inn lobby, yelling, "Lock the doors!" before collapsing.

Police arrived to find Saldivar in a pickup truck, pointing a gun at her own head. She surrendered after a nine-hour standoff. (Convicted of murder, she was sentenced to life in prison.) As with Elvis, Lennon, Morrison, and Cobain before her, the bumps and burrs of Selena's life and career were smoothed and sanitized by euphoric memory – and the machinery of celebrity marketing.

The creation of a cult requires magic. In Selena's case, a rumor crackled along the border that her black casket was empty. So her father-manager, Abraham, and mother, Marcela, allowed their daughter's body to be viewed by thirty thousand mourners, some from as far away as Japan, at the Bayfront Convention Center. (The family also publicized a 900 phone number at which the grieving could leave condolences – for $3.99 per call.)

The Selena following, fueled by the myth of the simple girl who goes from rags to riches while never forgetting her roots, was immediate and unstoppable. By the time her hearse arrived at Corpus Christi's Seaside Memorial Park for the internment, after a Jehovah's Witnesses funeral, hawkers were selling T-shirts bearing her likeness. Other items, such as Selena caps, shampoo, jewelry, pajamas, votary candles, and a hundred more mementos, followed. Selena's posthumous CD, *Dreaming of You*, eventually sold more than four million albums, becoming a crossover pop hit.

For at least a year, an average of a hundred visitors a day streamed into the cemetery from every point on the map. Each evening, truckloads of cards and flowers had to be carted away. Fans scrawled messages on the walls of the Days Inn room where the singer had met Saldivar and left flowers and cards on the fence of the modest house where Selena lived with her husband, Chris Perez. In the months following her death, six-hundred-plus baby girls in Texas alone were named Selena. And Governor George W. Bush declared her birthday, April 16, Selena Day.

Many Anglos failed to understand. On the day before the funeral, shock-jock Howard Stern played one of her songs overlaid with the sound of gunshots. (He later apologized in fractured Spanish.) *People* magazine didn't miss the message: After two hot-selling issues with Selena on the cover in the Southwest market, it launched *People en Español*, a successful Spanish-language spinoff.

Corpus Christi isn't Graceland, but a decade on, Selena still makes local cash registers ring. Thousands of visitors each year are handed maps to a variety of Selena sites. The current magnet is the life-size statue of their heroine on Shoreline Drive. The kiosk shading her bronze likeness was so often covered with scrawled messages that a controversial four-foot-high barrier now surrounds it. Some argue that Selena loved to be close to her fans and would

ABOVE AND BELOW: *The memorial in downtown Corpus Christi; a note left by a fan.*

have abhorred the railing, but her father, Abraham, said, "It was long overdue." The studio where Selena and her band recorded is now a museum, attracting a steady flow of visitors to view her red Porsche, awards, and skimpy sequined stage outfits. Ironically, though, the mainstream stardom that the Latina singer strove so hard to capture was finally achieved by Jennifer Lopez, who portrayed her in the 1997 biopic *Selena*. ✄

jackie wilson

June 9, 1934–January 21, 1984

Wilson died in near-poverty, but his admirers provided a lovely crypt and headstone.

With the likes of "Lonely Teardrops" and "(Your Love Keeps Lifting Me) Higher and Higher," Jackie Wilson scored five charttoppers between 1958 and 1963. The one-time Golden Gloves boxer's nickname, Mr. Excitement, came from his performances – unrelenting explosions of an athleticism that rivaled James Brown's, overlaid with a driving falsetto that sent female fans into full-tilt fits. Offstage, the handsome soul singer was literally a target for women. In 1961, a fan shot him in his New York City apartment. Wilson lost a kidney, and the bullet remained lodged in his body for the rest of his life. By 1975, his career had ebbed, and the Detroit native joined a Dick Clark nostalgia tour to pay his bills. While singing "Lonely Teardrops" at the Latin Casino in Cherry Hill, New Jersey, in September 1975, he was felled by a heart attack. Wilson collapsed, struck his head on the stage, and was knocked unconscious. Cornell Gunter of the Coasters tried to revive him until rescue workers arrived, but the oxygen deprivation to his brain was irreversible. Wilson remained comatose for a year, and then, when he became conscious, he was unable to talk and was partially paralyzed. He was moved to a Mt. Holly, New Jersey, nursing home, where he lived until his death eight years later.

The battle over his estate, and his person, began almost immediately after his hospitalization. Joyce McRae, a concerned Chicago friend, mounted a modest crusade to improve Wilson's minimal care, in which treatment was often denied by his insurance coverage through the American Federation of Television and Radio Artists (AFTRA). Meantime, Wilson's representatives were suspected of siphoning off his royalties. (His manager, Nat Tarnopol, was later convicted on federal charges of malfeasance.)

In a struggle that would go on from his demise through the present time, his estranged second wife, Harlean Harris, whom he never divorced, sued to become the administrator of the singer's estate. Lynn Crotchett, with whom Wilson had lived since 1970 but never married, also filed a claim. The estate, though, did finally win a settlement from AFTRA as part of a class-action suit. While the legal wrangling was in progress, Wilson's grave, in the blue-collar Detroit suburb of Wayne, went unmarked for three years, until friends in the music industry raised the money to fund the headstone and crypt that now grace the plot. ✄

BOBBY HATFIELD

August 10, 1940–November 5, 2003

"If there's a rock & roll heaven/Well you know they've got a hell of a band," sang the Righteous Brothers. On November 5, 2003, that celestial group got a new vocalist. Brother Bobby Hatfield, the passionate tenor of the duo, was found dead in his hotel room in Kalamazoo, Michigan, where the Brothers had booked a concert.

In the days before music videos, people were stunned when they saw the Righteous Brothers in person. How could two white guys from Orange County, California, sound that black? It was righteous, indeed. The pair produced a string of hits, including "(You're My) Soul and Inspiration," "Unchained Melody," and 1964's "You've Lost That Lovin' Feeling," the most programmed song in radio history. Hatfield and his partner Bill Medley broke up and reunited a few times, but through the decades their work remained visible, gracing the soundtracks of *Top Gun*, *Ghost*, and *Dirty Dancing*. Even as they entered their sixties, the Rock and Roll Hall of Famers kept a tour schedule. They were set to perform in Kalamazoo when Hatfield died of what initially appeared to be a heart attack brought on by advanced coronary disease. But toxicology tests revealed that his heart gave out due to "acute cocaine intoxication." There was speculation that Hatfield, who never seemed to have a drug problem, used cocaine to combat the fatigue his heart condition engendered. He was also under stress: His wife Linda had weathered years of suffering from Lupus and was recovering from cancer.

Hatfield was interred not far from his Newport Beach home at Pacific View Memorial Park in Corona del Mar, California. "He lived every moment until he died," said Medley, "and you can't ask for anything better than that." ✄

The Righteous Brother was interred near his Orange County home.

NICO
October 16, 1938–July 18, 1988

The Velvet Underground singer is buried in Berlin's Grunewald Forest.

With a jaded sophistication that went beyond a stage act, the troubled German model and singer Nico (née Christa Päffgen) once sang, "I came here to die with you." In the beginning, though, the Cologne-born beauty was full of life. She modeled for French *Vogue*, took acting lessons in the same class as Marilyn Monroe, had a small role in Fellini's *La Dolce Vita*, and hooked up in the 1960s with Andy Warhol and sang with the Velvet Underground, the seminal group that thumbed its nose at flower power with complex songs of alienation and deviancy. Nico added her own Teutonic monotone, devoid of color or emotion. On a tune Lou Reed wrote for her, she droned, "I'll be your mirror/ Reflect what you are in case you don't know." So she became. Billed as rock & roll's "Moon Goddess," she faded in and out of the scene with a few records and tours, and a string of lovers that included Jim Morrison and Brian Jones.

By the 1970s, heroin controlled her life and didn't let go for over a decade. A couple of years before her death, her methadone dependence was waning, and she seemed on her way to recovery. In 1988, she was riding a bicycle on the Spanish resort island of Ibiza when she collapsed and fell by the road. Taken to the island's Cannes Nisto Hospital, she was misdiagnosed as having had sunstroke, and she died the next day of a cerebral hemorrhage. Nico was cremated and her ashes taken to a small cemetery in the Grunewald Forest, a fairy-tale woods in Berlin. Her cremains were buried next to her mother, Margarete, while a few friends played her album *Desertshore* on a cassette recorder. "Death must have come upon her like an old friend," said her manager Alan Wise. "She was always toying with it. Life was a bore to her and rather wearisome." ❧

SID VICIOUS
May 10, 1957–February 2, 1979

NANCY SPUNGEN
February 27, 1958–October 12, 1978

Sid Vicious and Nancy Spungen were rock & roll's Bonnie and Clyde. In the late seventies, they cut a wide, drug-fueled swath through the nihilistic London punk scene before washing up in New York. Philadelphia-bred Spungen, an ex–New York Dolls groupie, psychologically disturbed since childhood, introduced the Sex Pistols' Vicious to heroin. The lovers careened through life at a tipping point of violence, separations, overdoses, and crippling codependence. They often said they wouldn't live to see twenty-one. By late 1978, Vicious (born John Simon Ritchie), an inept musician whose bass was often purposely unplugged by Sex Pistols roadies, had been jettisoned by the band and, managed by Spungen, was trying to mold a solo career. The couple resided at New York's bohemian Chelsea Hotel, where in the early hours of October 12, Vicious regained

consciousness from a morphine-fueled stupor in Room 100 to find Spungen dead on the bathroom floor. She had bled to death from a single stab wound in her stomach. The murder weapon was a seven-inch hunting knife the couple had recently bought to defend themselves from other addicts.

Many speculated that Sid stabbed Nancy in the midst of an argument and then passed out. Some thought she was killed by a drug dealer, and others believe her death was the result of the couple's suicide pact. In 1983, Nancy's mother, Deborah Spungen, published *And I Don't Want to Live This Life*. In the book, she claimed that the twenty-year-old engineered her own death: "She egged [Sid] into stabbing her by convincing him it was the only way he could prove his love for her."

Sid, who said he had no memory of the event, told the police, "I did it because I'm a dirty dog." But the truth would never be known. He soon made an attempt to kill himself, slashing his wrists with a razor blade and a broken light bulb, screaming, according to author Malcolm Butt, "I want to join Nancy; I didn't keep my part of the bargain." He was bailed out of Riker's Island where he was being

held for the murder but soon was back in jail. He slashed Todd Smith, brother of poet-musician Patti Smith, with a broken bottle in a club called Hurrah's. Freed again on February 1, Vicious celebrated with his mother, Ann Beverley, herself a former heroin addict who sometimes referred to Spungen as Nauseating Nancy, at the apartment of his new girlfriend Michelle Robinson. Sometime during the evening he injected heroin and was found dead in bed the next morning.

Vicious was cremated, and his ashes were scattered over Nancy's grave in Buck's County, Pennsylvania, against the wishes of her parents. They may have been together in death, but the legacy of their odd and agonizing love affair has dimmed since it first made headlines. After Nancy's demise, fashion designer Vivienne Westwood, partner of Sex Pistols impresario Malcolm McLaren, brought out Sid Vicious T-shirts emblazoned with SHE'S DEAD, I'M ALIVE, I'M YOURS. The 1986 movie *Sid and Nancy*, starring Gary Oldman and Chloe Webb, briefly revived interest in the pair. These days, though, Nancy's grave has an unkempt look and is rarely visited. ✂

The Sex Pistol's ashes were surreptitiously scattered on his girlfriend's grave.

Strawberry Fields Forever

JOHN LENNON
October 9, 1940–December 8, 1980

GEORGE HARRISON
February 25, 1943–November 29, 2001

Some believe that Yoko Ono scattered her husband's ashes at his memorial mosaic.

ohn Lennon was shot to death in New York City late last night. . . . I'm sorry if I can't regain my composure here. . . . I'm a little upset. . . ." The news bulletin, read by a Grand Rapids, Michigan, disc jockey, spoke to a worldwide loss of composure. Rock & roll's greatest innovator and surest master was gunned down in front of the exclusive Dakota apartment building by Mark David Chapman, an obsessed fan. Lennon was rushed in a police car to nearby Roosevelt Hospital, but one of the bullets had severed the left subclavian artery, and he was pronounced dead on arrival.

The ex-Beatle's end came not only with shocking suddenness but just as his creative life was looking up again. For five years, Lennon had almost disappeared into the Dakota, tending to his family and new son Sean, while second wife, Yoko Ono, handled their business affairs. But that fall, he appeared in the studio once more. He and Ono were returning from working on her single "Walking on Thin Ice" when he was murdered. He was holding a tape of the song when he fell.

The following day, Ono issued a terse statement: "There is no funeral for John. John loved and prayed for the human race. Please pray the same for him." Without even a memorial service for close friends, Lennon's body was cremated at Ferndale Crematory in suburban Ardsley, New York.

Such haste was bound to create an unpleasant stir. According to controversial biographer Albert Goldman, Lennon feared cremation. Goldman also claimed that the singer's family in England was not consulted about the arrangements. When the cremains were given to Ono, conjecture ran wild: She scattered the ashes in Central Park; she kept them on the mantle; under her bed. Wisely, she has never said exactly where her husband's ashes are. As with rockers from Elvis to Morrison to Allman, any location would surely become a target for fanatics. On "Thin Ice" Ono sings, "And when our hearts return to ashes/It'll be just a story."

It became, of course, a saga. A week after the murder, 100,000 people gathered in the chilly gloom outside the Dakota to pay their respects. They were joined by millions around the world. Sparked by Ono's gift of one million dollars, New York City created a 2.5-acre tear-drop-shaped area of Central Park near the Dakota, dedicated to peace. Strawberry Fields, named after the Beatles' song, attracts two to three million visitors a year, and on Lennon anniversaries, hundreds gather to light candles and sing "Imagine" and "Give Peace a Chance" around the circular mosaic. The memorial also has become true north for vigils and rallies of all kinds. Deadheads gathered there when Jerry Garcia died, and fans returned to mourn George Harrison's death.

Lennon's killer, meanwhile, has remained incarcerated. At his third unsuccessful parole hearing in 2004, Chapman said that he wanted to "steal" Lennon's fame. But admitted, "I'm a bigger nobody than I was before."

Not so his victim. A quarter of a century on, Lennon still ranks fourth on the *Forbes* magazine list of top-earning dead celebrities, with an annual take of $21 million. Harrison is seventh with $7 million. Lennon's legacy has even helped bring his hometown out of decades of economic and social decline. Liverpool's rebirth is driven by tourism, much of it Beatles-related. The English industrial center features an annual Beatles Week, nightly performances at the reconstructed Cavern Club (where the

A memento left shortly after Lennon's death

group first played), and a museum that boasts a mock-up of a 1960 Hamburg street, like the one where the quartet first honed its skills. God only knows what Lennon would have made of the biggest honor: The newly humming Liverpool John Lennon Airport. It uses his famous sketched self-portrait as its logo. Its motto: "Above Us Only Sky."

"Nothing in this life that I've been trying/ Could equal or surpass the art of dying," wrote George Harrison. After he contracted cancer in 1997, the guitarist planned for a graceful exit. Following the diagnosis, Harrison, a longtime convert to Eastern spirituality and the Krishna religion, remained ensconced at Friar Park, his sprawling estate in Oxfordshire, England. He worked on music with his son, Dhani, and spent hours at his favorite pastime, gardening. Two years later, however, he almost met his end at the hands of Michael Abram, a deranged man who had broken into the Harrison mansion. Abram stabbed Harrison, almost fatally, before his wife Olivia bashed the attacker over the head with a fireplace poker.

As cancer spread from his lungs to his brain, Harrison sought treatment in Switzerland. He bought a villa in Montagnola, where he worked in the rose gardens when he was able. By the summer of 2001, the treatments weren't helping, so the family moved to New York, where Harrison, by then wheelchair-bound when he could get out of bed, underwent radical radiation therapy from controversial oncologist Dr. Gil Lederman. In the middle of treatment, the failing musician was subjected to a cruel indignity. Lederman apparently coerced the gravely ill man to sign a guitar for his son as well as autographs for his daughters. (Harrison's estate later sued the doctor but dropped the action when he surrendered the guitar.)

Harrison's main concerns were that his passage to the next life would accord with Krishna religious traditions and that his final resting place would remain secret and undisturbed. Many assumed he would go to his remote Hawaiian estate at the end, or to the home of his friend Gavin de Becker, security man to the stars. But three days before he died, according to a 2002 English news account, he was secretly flown to Los Angeles, where he stayed at 9536 Heather Road in Beverly Hills, an estate Paul McCartney had recently bought from Courtney Love. As two Krishna devotees chanted, he died quietly, with his family at his bedside.

Harrison was hastily cremated in a $650 ceremony at the Hollywood Forever Cemetery and Crematorium, final resting place of Rudolph Valentino and Cecil B. DeMille. A Hare Krishna priest read Hindu verses over the flower-strewn simple wooden coffin before it was consigned to the flames. His ashes were given to Olivia, who respected her husband's wish for secrecy. Most think his ashes were scattered in the Ganges at the holy Indian city of Varanasi; some say in northern India's Yamuna River. Others believe that they were strewn on his beloved rose beds in Montagnola or are somewhere at Friar Park. "Life is one long enigma, my friend," he sang. "So read on, read on/The answer's at the end." ✄

OPPOSITE PAGE: *Harrison's death prompted instant memorials at Strawberry Fields.*

JERRY GARCIA
August 1, 1942–August 9, 1995

The long, strange trip continued even after Jerry Garcia's death. The Grateful Dead guitarist – and psychedelic shaman to multiple generations – died in his sleep of a heart attack at Serenity Knolls rehabilitation center, not far from his Marin County, California, home. He had checked in two days earlier to be treated for drug addiction. The reaction to his death created odd juxtapositions: An announcement of his demise flashed on the news crawl at the New York Stock Exchange, while a tie-dyed flag flew at half-mast over San Francisco City Hall. Thousands of Deadheads set up an impromptu memorial at the corner of Haight and Ashbury, and in New York, the faithful flocked to Central Park's Strawberry Fields. Record stores across the country quickly sold out of Dead CDs, and grocery stores were picked clean of Ben & Jerry's Cherry Garcia ice cream. President Clinton, a fan of Garcia-designed neckties, told MTV he was saddened by the passing of the icon.

At Garcia's funeral at St. Stephen's Episcopal Church in Belvedere, an upscale San Francisco suburb, the shaky-voiced guitarist was laid out in an open coffin, dressed in a black T-shirt, sweatpants, and a windbreaker. Along with family and friends, Bob Dylan, novelist Ken Kesey, and basketball star Bill Walton were on hand for what became a joyous celebration. Music was made by the surviving Dead, and their departed frontman was given a standing ovation. "I want everyone to know," said his third, and final, wife, filmmaker Deborah Koons Garcia, "that he died with a smile on his face." There was one sour note, though.

Annabelle Garcia, the musician's daughter with second wife, Carolyn "Mountain Girl" Adams Garcia, said of her dad: "He was a shitty father and a great man."

The trip then turned especially bizarre. Garcia, per his wishes, was cremated. He had often said he wanted his ashes scattered at sea, but widow Deborah and the Dead's Bob Weir had other ideas. They secretly flew to India and scattered some of Garcia's cremains in the Ganges. On the riverbank, Weir strummed a Dead signature tune, "Friend of the Devil," but was too overcome with tears to finish.

Back in Marin County, Carolyn and Garcia's four daughters were enraged, mistakenly believing that all of the ashes had been scattered. "There was no reason on earth to take Jerry's ashes to India, a country he's never been to and dump them in the most polluted river on the face of the earth," said Carolyn. Finally, on August 15, friends and family boarded the *Argosy Venture* in San Francisco to take the remaining ashes out to sea. Before the ketch could set sail, though, Deborah adamantly refused to let Carolyn onboard. Weir tried to reason with Deborah, to no avail. (The two women remained enemies, battling in court until 2001, when Carolyn was awarded a share of Garcia's reportedly $12 million estate.) As Carolyn was left standing forlornly on the pier, Weir almost dived off the boat because the situation was so "un-Jerry," he later said. After the craft passed the Golden Gate Bridge into the open sea, those who so desired reached into the plastic bag and scattered Garcia's remaining ashes into the Pacific. ✄

T. Rex

marc bolan
September 30, 1947–September 16, 1977

steve peregrin took
July 28, 1949–October 27, 1980

Marc Bolan and his 1970s glam-rock group T. Rex never reached superstar status in the United States. But the charismatic singer with the cherubic ringlets was a smash act in his native Britain, where he commanded a Beatlesque following. So it is perhaps no wonder that he has three grave markers there. After T. Rex became extinct in 1975, Bolan told *Rolling Stone*, "I was living in a twilight world of drugs, booze, and kinky sex." That lifestyle cocktail came to an abrupt end in the foggy early hours of September 16, 1977, when Bolan and his girlfriend, American singer Gloria Jones, left a Mayfair restaurant, heading home. Their purple Mini Clubman, with Jones at the wheel, smashed into a tree beside London's Queen's Ride Street. Bolan, 29, was killed instantly. After recovering from injuries, Jones returned to America with their son, Rolan Bolan (now a singer and Tommy Hilfiger model). She was accused of drunk driving but never returned to England to face the charge.

The likes of David Bowie and Rod Stewart attended Bolan's funeral, but the highlight of the service was a lavish bouquet of flowers shaped into a swan, in remembrance of his song "Ride a White Swan." Bolan, whose birth name was Mark Feld, was cremated and his ashes scattered at London's venerable Golders Green Crematorium, where the remains of such notables as Sigmund Freud also rest. Upon their later deaths, the ashes of Bolan's parents, Simeon and Phyllis Feld, were scattered in the same location as their son's. Two plaques honoring the rocker are attached to the wall of Golders Green Mausoleum. One of them hangs next to a plaque for Who drummer Keith Moon, who died in 1978. The other was erected by Bolan's fan club. On the anniversary of his death, hundreds of devotees gather at the cemetery and at the crash site, where they leave notes and swan figurines at the base of the tree. The tree memorial is maintained by fans calling themselves T.A.G. (T. Rex Action Group). On the twenty-fifth anniversary of his death, in 2002, Rolan Bolan unveiled a bronze bust of his father at the site.

T. Rex cofounder Steve Peregrin Took, buried in another London cemetery, suffered a far less glamorous coda three years after Bolan's demise. While high on morphine, he choked to death on a cocktail cherry. ✖

Born Mark Feld, Bolan shares a resting place with his parents.

Fans decorate Bolan's bust at the tree where he died in a car crash and where there is a bulletin board of sorts upon which to leave notes and photos.

KEITH MOON
'WHO' drummer
1946 – 1978
"There is no substitute"

IN RESPECTFUL MEMORY
OF
MARC BOLAN
(BORN: MARK FELD)
30th SEPTEMBER, 1947.
16th SEPTEMBER, 1977.
MUSICIAN, WRITER AND POET.
MUCH LOVED AND MISSED
BY HIS FANS
AND ALL THOSE WHOSE
LIVES HE TOUCHED.

IN
LOVING
MEMORY
OF
MARC BOLAN
30.09.47 - 16.09.77
"25 YEARS ON HIS LIGHT OF
LOVE STILL SHINES BRIGHTLY"
PLACED BY THE OFFICIAL
MARC BOLAN FAN CLUB AND
FELLOW FANS TO COMMEMORATE
THE 25TH ANNIVERSARY
OF HIS PASSING
SEPTEMBER 2002

STEPHEN ROSS PORTER
(STEVE PEREGRIN TOOK)
28. 7. 1949 ~ 27. 10. 1980

MUSICIAN
LOVED AND REMEMBERED

ABOVE: *T. Rex cofounder Steve Peregrin Took (né Stephen Ross Porter) died at age thirty-one.*

OPPOSITE PAGE: *Plaques dedicated to Marc Bolan at Golders Green Crematorium in London*

KEITH MOON
August 23, 1946–September 7, 1978

*I*nstead of the usual floral arrangement for the funeral of his band mate Keith Moon, singer Roger Daltrey sent a TV set with a champagne bottle protruding from its shattered screen. Good choice. After all, the Who drummer wasn't known as Moon the Loon for nothing. He never drove a Lincoln Continental into a Holiday Inn swimming pool as he often bragged, and it's unlikely that he was once paralyzed for days after taking a horse tranquilizer. But for almost a decade before his death, the self-taught stickman was Britain's official wildman: trashing cars, homes, hotels, and restaurants with alcohol-fueled élan. Onstage, his antics were the norm. The Who was known for smashing their instruments at concert end, and Moon loaded his drums with flash powder. Once he overdid it,

and the resulting explosion left cuts on his legs and singed lead guitarist Pete Townshend's hair. Behind the sparks, though, Moon's demolition-derby style on songs like "I Can See for Miles" and on the rock opera *Tommy* brought rock drumming from metronomic time-keeping to center-stage performance.

Years of drug and alcohol abuse, however, overshadowed Moon's talent. On September 6, 1978, he attended a première party for the movie *The Buddy Holly Story*, thrown by Paul and Linda McCartney at a London restaurant. He happily told the couple that he was engaged to his companion, Swedish actress Annette Walter-Lax. Back at his rented flat on Curzon Lane (the same one in which Mama Cass Elliot had died in 1974), he downed several tablets of Heminevrin, a psychoactive muscle relaxant prescribed to help with alcohol withdrawal. He slept for a few hours, awoke, and downed more of the drug. He had also done some drinking, a no-no with Heminevrin, and snorted some cocaine. Later, Walter-Lax found him face down on the floor. He was pronounced dead at Middlesex Hospital, and his death was later ruled due to accidental respiratory failure.

More than a hundred people crowded into the small West Chapel of London's Golders Green Crematorium for Moon's funeral. Along with Daltrey, Townshend, and Who bassist John Entwistle, fellow rockers Eric Clapton, Charlie Watts, and Bill Wyman were among the mourners. Before Moon was cremated and his ashes scattered in the cemetery, Daltrey kidded that the whole thing might be one of Moon's practical jokes. He told a friend that he half expected Moon to jump out of the coffin and go, "Ha, ha, fooled you." ✂

The Who drummer flamed out in death as well as in life; his ashes were scattered at Golders Green Crematorium.

mick RONSON

May 26, 1946–April 29, 1993

Michael "Mick" Ronson's third and last solo album was appropriately titled *Heaven 'n Hull*. The acclaimed guitarist hailed from Hull, in northeast England, and in the pantheon of glam-rock stars his playing was paradise. Ronson came to prominence leading David Bowie's Spiders From Mars band and did double duty on the classic *Ziggy Stardust* album, which he both played on and helped produce. During his later solo career, he served as lead guitar for Bob Dylan's Rolling Thunder Revue and produced such artists as John Mellencamp, Lou Reed, and Morrissey. He began working on *Heaven 'n Hull* after learning in 1991 that he had liver cancer. Bowie, Mellencamp, and Ronson's old mates Ian Hunter (Mott the Hoople) and Joe Elliott (Def Leppard) joined in on vocals and instrumentals. Ronson died before the album was finished; it was issued a year later. The guitarist, a Mormon, was buried in his hometown, next to his father, George. Later that year, Bowie told Arsenio Hall on his talk show, "Of all the early-seventies guitar players, Mick was probably one of the most influential and profound, and I miss him a lot." ✀

Ronson had a Mormon funeral and was buried in his hometown of Hull, England.

JOHN BONHAM

May 31, 1948–September 25, 1980

Led Zeppelin's John "Bonzo" Bonham was the Evel Knievel of percussion: His every performance was like jumping over ten cars. His backbeat powered the pioneering English quartet, and his signature drum solo, "Moby Dick," set heavy-metal style. Bonham screamed while he played, and he lived at full volume as well. Increasingly, though, alcohol was not only his recreation but his ruin. At one of Zeppelin's last appearances in 1977, he was so smashed he fell off his drum stool during the third song. On September 24, 1980, Bonham left his Worcestershire farm, the Old Hyde, where he lived with his wife Pat and their two children, to rehearse at a nearby studio. Bonham drank heavily during the day and continued that evening, when the group gathered at the Windsor home of lead guitarist Jimmy Page. Late that night, Bonham passed out and was put to bed on his side with his head propped up, according to testimony at the coroner's inquest. When he didn't appear the next morning, Zeppelin tour manager Benji LeFevre found him on his back, choked to death on aspirated vomit.

After a funeral at the Rushock parish church near his farm, Bonham was buried in the sanctuary's modest cemetery, as sheep bleated in the adjoining pasture. His remote resting place is not a major stop on Zeppelin fan pilgrimages, yet the church's guest book holds some names of visitors from all over Europe, America, and Japan. Led Zeppelin never successfully re-formed after Bonham's death, but his own family has continued his musical bent. Younger sister Debbie Bonham is a singer; his son Jason plays drums with various rock groups, and daughter Zoe Bonham's solo guitar-vocal act is gaining notice in the U.K. ✄

OPPOSITE PAGE: *Drumsticks are among the mementos left at the bucolic English grave of the Led Zeppelin percussionist.*

RICK NeLSON
May 8, 1940–December 31, 1985

Rick Nelson was born with musical bloodlines: Father Ozzie was a former big-band leader and mother Harriet a 1930s songbird. Ricky, as he was called, was raised on a Hollywood soundstage along with his older brother, David, as a member of "America's Favorite Family." The Nelsons ruled radio and TV by playing themselves on *The Adventures of Ozzie and Harriet*, and Ricky became a teen heartthrob for millions of young viewers. They snapped up his first single, a cover of Fats Domino's "I'm Walkin'," to the tune of a million copies. Nelson unwittingly helped to popularize rock & roll in the 1950s by giving it mass exposure on the family's television show. Twelve years later, when he tried to play new songs rather than his early hits, he was booed at a Madison Square Garden concert, an experience that resulted in the lyrics to his 1972 hit "Garden Party."

Although Nelson loved to perform, he was forced to spend an average of 250 exhausting nights per year on tour during the early 1980s. His acrimonious, drawn-out divorce from Kris Harmon (sister of actor Mark Harmon), the mother of his four children, was draining him psychologically and financially. Just months before his death, his twin blond sons, Gunnar and Matthew, who now perform as the singing duo Nelson, and his daughter Tracy, who became an actress, came to live with Rick to escape their alcoholic mother. On New Year's Eve, Rick boarded his DC-3 (previously owned by Jerry Lee Lewis) in Guntersville, Alabama, headed for a date in Dallas. Three hours into the flight, the pilot reported trouble onboard; he was going down. The plane crashed near DeKalb, Texas, and blazed up into an inferno. The pilots escaped through the cockpit windows, but Nelson, his four-man Stone Canyon Band, his soundman, and his fiancée, Helen Blair, burned to death. Rumors circulated that Nelson and his band were freebasing cocaine on their plane, which caused it to catch fire. But the Federal Aviation Administration ruled that a faulty heating system was behind the explosion.

After a private funeral in Los Angeles, Nelson was laid to rest in Forest Lawn-Hollywood Hills cemetery, near his father's site (Harriet was buried there in 1994). Rick's grave is also close to those of R&B singer Esther Phillips and singing cowboy Roy Rogers's movie sidekick Gabby Hayes. Groundskeepers say that to this day they often have to clean lipstick prints from Rick's marker. ✄

The son of the famous TV family lies near his parents, Ozzie and Harriet.

CLYDE McPHATTER

November 15, 1932–June 13, 1972

McPhatter's grave is easy to miss at the George Washington Cemetery, in Paramus, New Jersey.

When Clyde McPhatter formed the vocal group the Drifters in 1953, he recruited several members from Harlem's Mount Lebanon Singers, bringing the emotional ecstasy of gospel to R&B. A keystone in the creation of soul, the Drifters churned out doo-wop hits including "Money Honey," "Such a Night," and "Whatcha Gonna Do," before McPhatter was drafted into the Army in 1954. The quartet would sail on for more than two decades, with several complete changes of personnel. After his discharge from the service, McPhatter scored with solo hits including "A Lover's Question" and "Long Lonely Nights." But as his career waned in the 1960s, he began drinking heavily, and his Atlantic Records contract was not renewed. "It wasn't the same Clyde McPhatter," said Atlantic chief Jerry Wexler. Although he was married, it is believed that near the end of his life McPhatter took up with a woman known only as Bertha, who became his drinking buddy until he died from a heart attack. A Rock and Roll Hall of Famer inducted for both solo and group careers, McPhatter was buried under a simple bronze marker in a Paramus, New Jersey, cemetery.

His widow, Lena, found herself without benefits from the American Federation of Television and Radio Artists (AFTRA). At the time, to be eligible for AFTRA's twenty thousand dollars in death assistance, the late artist would have had to have earned a minimum of five thousand dollars the preceding year, which McPhatter did not. "[Lena] wasn't getting paid by anybody," said Chuck Rubin, a New York artist representative who took her case. "Eventually I got her paid, and today she's all right. But it took years." ✄

A Mama and a Papa

"mama" cass eLLiot

September 19, 1941–July 29, 1974

"papa" JOHN PHILLIPS

August 30, 1935–March 18, 2001

No, Mama Cass did not choke to death on a ham sandwich. Rock & roll's premiere urban myth has persisted for three decades and can still be found in some biographical sketches. The reality is less dramatic, and more touching. Cass Elliot, the ample contralto of the Mamas and the Papas – the "California Dreamin' " quartet whose tie-dyed harmonies dominated pop charts in the 1960s – succumbed to a heart attack at age thirty-two.

She had been developing a promising solo career and had been performing in London when she died in the flat she rented from songwriter Harry Nilsson at 9 Curzon Place. (Four years later, the Who's drummer Keith Moon would die of an overdose in the same apartment.) There was no mystery about the cause of Elliot's demise. Only five feet five, she weighed more than 230 pounds. London coroner Keith Simpson found that she had suffered "heart failure due to fatty myocardial

degeneration due to obesity." There was no sign, he noted, of food blocking her trachea. "Her death wasn't surprising," said Mama Michelle Phillips, who was devastated by Elliot's demise. "She didn't take care of herself. She'd lose a hundred pounds and gain it back again."

The singer's funeral at Hollywood Memorial Park was marred by out-of-control fans. "I was actually frightened for our personal safety," said her sister Leah Kunkel, a lawyer. "Our limousine was mobbed." Elliot was the last person cremated at the Park, the final resting place of Peter Lorre and Rudolph Valentino, before it closed its gates. (It reopened as Hollywood Forever in 1999, with tens of thousands of new plots.) Elliot's ashes were buried in her native Baltimore, but around 1990, they were moved to L.A.'s Mount Sinai Memorial Park. There, her site was more accessible to her daughter, Owen Elliot, who, upon visiting, placed a

Papa John succumbed to liver cancer and was buried in Palm Springs, California.

token pebble on the headstone – a Jewish tradition intended to console others who visit the grave.

Papa John Phillips, the Grammy-winning group's architect, was odd man out in a tense love triangle that caused the group to dissolve in 1971. While Phillips partied and slid slowly into a thousand-dollar-per-day heroin and cocaine habit, his wife and protégée Michelle had an intense affair with Papa Denny Doherty. Elliot, too, pined for Doherty; the atmosphere became poisonous. Phillips, who also wrote songs for the Grateful Dead and the Beach Boys, entered rehab in 1980, following an arrest for distributing drugs. "I have no idea what my music would've been like without the drugs," he said. "What would the Titanic have been like if it hadn't sunk?" He was never again in robust health. In 1992, he had a liver transplant followed by two hip replacements. His final illness, a stomach infection that his body could not battle, brought him to the UCLA Medical Center. As he worsened, his fourth wife, Farnaz, refused to let Michelle see her former husband, until manager Lou Adler and Doherty interceded. "When I stood there looking at him . . . everything we had been through was gone," she recalled. "He gave me a kiss and said, 'Mich, I want you to come and see me again.' But he was dead by the next day." After a brief service, attended by Phillips's daughters, Mackenzie, of *One Day at a Time* fame; Chynna, of the group Wilson Phillips; and model-actress Bijou, the singer was buried beneath a simple bronze plaque at Palm Springs Mortuary. In the end, his passing was pure California. Chynna said on the day after her father died, "I spent the morning with my sisters. We are all on our way to the beach, where we will walk and swim and celebrate our father's life." ✄

Mama Cass died of a heart attack in the same London flat owned by Harry Nilsson in which Keith Moon died.

SHANNON HOON

September 26, 1967–October 21, 1995

They call themselves Melonheads. Every year in late September, several hundred of them converge on tiny Dayton, Indiana, a speck on the map halfway between Chicago and Indianapolis. They come for a vigil at the grave of Shannon Hoon, the Blind Melon frontman who died of an accidental drug overdose at age twenty-eight. Their devotion is as perplexing as it is touching. Blind Melon burned briefly in the early nineties with just one heavily promoted single, "No Rain," and two albums. And Hoon is hardly a posthumous Lizard King, trailing clouds of charisma from the tomb. But that, ironically, seems to be the attraction. Hoon, said fan and repeat vigil attendee Tad Grabnick, an Illinois art teacher, "is no one-hit wonder. I think the media sold him out."

I KNOW WE CAN'T ALL STAY HERE FOREVER SO I WANT TO WRITE MY WORDS ON THE FACE OF TODAY AND THEY'LL PAINT IT.

The "happening," on the weekend nearest Hoon's September 26 birthday, first gathered steam on the Internet, and now fans, many whom were in grade school when Blind Melon was on the charts, make the journey from as far away as Singapore and Serbia. The Hoon family, all from nearby Lafayette, which is also the home of Axl Rose, has stayed intensely involved in the ritual. Shannon's mother, Nell, decorates the grave with candles, roses, and pictures, to which guests add their own homages. "They're really a wonderful group of kids," she said in an interview. "I'm sure Shannon knows they're there." Over the years, Nell has put up visitors in her home, even attending the weddings of youngsters who met at her son's grave. The intense personal connections are the magnet of the annual watch. Grace Quattrocki, Hoon's niece, decked out in her uncle's McCutcheon High School letter jacket and proudly sporting the turquoise necklace he wore for the band's *Rolling Stone* cover shoot, told a reporter, "I was only five when he died, but I bet if I knew him, we'd be best friends." ✂

Hoon's fans leave handwritten lyrics that echo those on his tombstone.

jam masteR jay

January 21, 1965–October 30, 2002

*L*aid out at the J. Foster Phillips Funeral Home near the Queens, New York, neighborhood where he was raised, Jam Master Jay (né Jason Mizell) was dressed in his trademark outfit: black leather suit, broad-brimmed black hat, and the loosely laced white Adidas with the three black stripes. Fans lined up for blocks in a cold rain for the viewing. "He was," said fellow hip-hop artist George "DJ Scratch" Spivey, "our John Lennon." Like the Beatle, Jay condemned violence, and like Lennon, he was shockingly and senselessly gunned down. A pair of masked assailants broke into his Queens recording studio and fatally shot him in the head. And like the Beatles, Jay and his two band mates

of the seminal trio Run-D.M.C. transformed pop music. The pioneering group was the first to successfully fuse rap and rock, one of the first hip-hop acts to go platinum, and the first to appear on mainstream magazine covers and be praised for its nonviolent repertoire. One of the many turntable- and album-shaped floral displays at Jay's star-studded funeral read: LOVE. RESPECT. L.L. COOL J, STUDENT.

At the funeral in Queens's Greater Allen Cathedral, mourners including Russell Simmons and Queen Latifah listened to Rev. Donnie McClurkin deliver the song "Stand." In his eulogy, Joseph Simmons, Run of Run-D.M.C., concluded, "I don't know if I should say this, but I believe this is Jason's biggest hit ever. It's his last DJ gig – here today."

Jay's death was an eerie echo of the violent 1990s, when rappers Tupac Shakur and Notorious B.I.G., famously antagonistic toward each other, were shot to death in separate incidents. Both murders remain unsolved. (Both men were cremated, and neither has a known grave marker.) Gestures of peace, however, were made at Jay's graveside service in Hartsdale, New York. Jay's three children, Jason, Terry, and Jesse, accompanied by mom Terri Corley-Mizell, each released a white dove.

As of this writing, Jay's murder remains an open case. Lawmen have investigated theories that the homicide was the result of a life insurance scam, a love triangle, or a drug deal. All have been dead ends. "I know justice will be done in God's own time," said Jay's mother, Connie Mizell. "He knows who did it, and that's the best person to know, because He'll deal with them." ✄

At his lavish funeral, a Run-D.M.C. pal said, "This may be Jason's biggest hit ever."

terry kath
January 31, 1946–January 23, 1978

TERRY ALAN KATH

1946 — 1978

COMPOSER — GUITARIST — SINGER

THE "MEMORIES OF LOVE" HE LEFT ON
EARTH, ALL THE WORLD HAS SHARED.
RARE AND GIFTED, GENTLE MAN WHOSE
RICHES WERE A SYMPHONY OF SONGS FOR
YOUNG AND OLD BECAUSE HE CARED.

♫ OUR LOVED ONE ♫

The Chicago guitarist is buried in Glendale, California.

Don't worry, it's not loaded." Terry Kath's last words have understandably found a place in rock & roll apocrypha. Kath was the cofounder, songwriter, and dazzling lead guitarist of Chicago, the brassed-up band that sold more than a hundred million records and dominated easy-listening airplay in the seventies and eighties. On January 23, 1978, the thirty-two-year-old Malibu, California, resident was drinking with his wife Camelia and his pal Don Johnson, a Chicago roadie who lived nearby. He had brought two handguns with him to Johnson's home, a .38 caliber revolver and a 9mm automatic. That was not unusual for the longtime gun collector. "I do target shooting, but I prefer just to go out into the desert and shoot at beer cans," he once said.

Kath was fooling around, playing pretend Russian roulette. He put the .38 to his temple and pulled the trigger several times. As he started to repeat the stunt with the automatic, Johnson asked him not to; it was making him nervous. Kath uttered his famous line, pulled the trigger, and died instantly. His death was ruled "accidental gunshot wound . . . under the influence of alcohol and drugs."

Some four hundred friends, family members, and musicians attended the funeral at Forest Lawn Memorial Park in Glendale, California. Recordings from Chicago's recent albums were played, and keyboardist Robert Lamm, standing by the rose-draped coffin, read from Kahlil Gibran's *The Prophet*. Kath's friend the Reverend Joe Burke said to mourners, including then-governor Jerry Brown and *Tonight Show* bandleader Doc Severinsen, "Someone said Terry's probably jamming with the late rock guitarist Jimi Hendrix right now. . . . I sure hope so." ✄

BIANCA HALSTEAD
May 5, 1965–December 15, 2001

BIANCA
BORN TO LOVE,
LIVED TO ROCK
May 5, 1965 - Dec. 15, 2001
We Love You
FOREVER

Given her balls-to-the-wall performances, it seemed certain that Bianca Halstead, lead singer of the Hollywood punk-glam band Betty Blowtorch, would flame out over sex, drugs, or rock & roll. After all, the spiky anthems by Blowtorch's heavily tattooed female members include "Are You Man Enough?," "Party Til' Ya Puke," and "Changing Underwear." But there was another side to Halstead. Despite her scary, anything-goes image, she had been sober and drug-free for a decade thanks to a twelve-step program. She was close to her parents, Angele and Gerry Woolery, as well as her two sisters and brother. In the wee hours after a performance and a night out in New Orleans, Halstead accepted a ride with acquaintance Brian McAllister. His 1986 Corvette was going over one hundred miles per hour when it spun out of control and was sideswiped on the passenger side by another vehicle. Halstead was killed instantly. (McAllister, whom police said had been drinking, faced criminal charges.)

An impromptu memorial formed at Serious, a clothing boutique on L.A.'s Melrose Avenue where Halstead sometimes worked. Fans and pals brought flowers and pictures, lit candles, and remembered the singer. She was cremated at Hollywood Forever Cemetery. Her ashes were placed in a Kiss lunchbox, which was enclosed in a case on wheels, the kind bands use to transport equipment. A Webcast of the ceremony, attended by L.A. punk's A list and with Halstead's pink bass guitar on hand, could be viewed at hollywoodforever.com. The sentiments on her marker in the cemetery's Garden of Legends section were echoed by her friend Rikki Rocket, the drummer for Poison. "In spite of her image, she was a loving, humble, kind soul who would totally go out of her way for people," he said. "She wanted to make people rock, smile, and forget." ✄

The funeral of the L.A. punk rocker was Webcast on the cemetery's Internet site. Her marker is one of the more spectacular in Hollywood Forever.

SONNY BONO
February 16, 1935–January 5, 1998

F Scott Fitzgerald was famously wrong when he said there are no second acts in American lives. Sonny Bono enjoyed at least three. As a singer/songwriter, his "I Got You Babe" and "The Beat Goes On" made Sonny and Cher a dynamic folk-rock duo on pop charts in the 1960s and stars of a TV variety show in the 1970s. After the couple divorced and the act dimmed, Bono turned his back on show biz to become a successful restaurateur. In 1988, upset about zoning laws that affected his eatery, he ran for mayor of Palm Springs. He won, and six years later he was elected to represent California's 44th District. "The last thing in the world I thought I would be is a U.S. congressman," the conservative Republican joked at a press dinner, "given all the bobcat vests and Eskimo boots I used to wear." An effective two-term lawmaker, he sat on both the House Judiciary and the National Security committees and was the most requested speaker at fund-raisers after his mentor Newt Gingrich.

In early 1998, after he failed to return from a solo ski run in South Lake Tahoe, a rescue team found Bono's body at the base of a lodgepole pine. Hitting the tree on a downhill run, he died from massive head injuries. Upon his demise, the flag atop the U.S. Capitol flew at half-mast, and his star on Palm Springs' main drag was heaped with flowers. Hundreds lined up to pay their respects at St. Theresa Catholic Church. One woman held her vintage Sonny and Cher dolls as she passed the coffin. Mourners including former President Gerald Ford and California governor Pete Wilson listened to Cher deliver a heartfelt eulogy that repaired decades of public sniping. Sonny, she said, "had the confidence to be the butt of the joke because he created the joke."

After he was laid to rest in nearby Cathedral City, friends gathered at Bono's home. Said his fourth wife, Mary, who would finish her husband's congressional term and be twice reelected, "Sonny would have loved this: seventy-five people in the kitchen to cook for, and lots of great press." Within a year, she drew media attention of her own, telling *TV Guide* that Bono took "fifteen, twenty" Vicodin and Valium pills per day for chronic back and neck pain. "I'm 100 percent convinced that is why he died," she said. "What he did showed an absolute lack of judgment. That's what these pills do." Bono's autopsy, however, showed no signs of alcohol or drug use. ✄

Gerald Ford and Cher both attended the congressman's funeral.

aNDY ǤIBB

March 5, 1958–March 10, 1988

I always knew that one day I'd get a call like this," said Kim Reeder, ex-wife of Andy Gibb, when she was informed of his death. "It was only a matter of time." In the beginning, the clock didn't tick so fast. The Australian teen heartthrob was born with a golden guitar in his hands. His three older brothers were the bell-bottomed Bee Gees. By the time Gibb was twenty-one, he had been nominated for two Grammys, sold 15 million records, and was the only solo performer ever to have his first three singles – "I Just Want to Be Your Everything," "(Love Is) Thicker than Water," and "Shadow Dancing" – top the charts.

As his celebrity accelerated, so did a prodigious cocaine habit. Gibb eventually lost his recording contracts, his money, and his gig as host of the musical variety show *Solid Gold*. The last straw was when actress girlfriend Victoria Principal left him. "I started to do cocaine around the clock," he later said. "I really think the major reason I fell from stardom was my affair with Victoria." For her part, Principal told *People* magazine, "Our breakup was preceded and precipitated by Andy's use of drugs. I did everything I could to help him." Finally, a phone conversation with recovering addict Elizabeth Taylor persuaded Gibb to enter the Betty Ford Clinic.

Afterward, while working on an album, Gibb lived at the lavish English estate of Bee Gee brother Robin. Two days after quietly celebrating his thirtieth birthday, he was admitted to Radcliffe Hospital in Oxford, complaining of stomach pains. On March 10, at 8:30 a.m., Andy was told that more tests were needed. "Fine," he said. A few moments later he slumped into unconsciousness and died. Though many speculated that cocaine was the cause, a terse statement from the hospital reported, "Mr. Gibb died from inflammation of the heart of the sort commonly caused by a virus. There is no evidence that his death was related to drink or drugs."

Family and friends attended Gibb's funeral at Forest Lawn-Hollywood Hills Cemetery, after which he was interred in the wall of its mausoleum. In 1998, brother Maurice (who died in 2003 and has no known marker) said that Andy's death brought the three surviving siblings closer and made them appreciate life. "At that funeral," he said, "we made [a] pact that we can't let anything come between us, and take life as it is – have fun." ⁑

Andy Gibb's Bee Gee brother Maurice has no known grave.

The Temptations

david ruffin
January 18, 1941–June 1, 1991

melvin franklin
October 12, 1942–February 23, 1995

paul williams
July 2, 1939–August 17, 1973

eddie kendricks
December 17, 1939–October 5, 1992

How could there be a Temptations curse? With gospel-honed harmonies and sugar-smooth choreography, the Temptations are one of the most successful male vocal groups in rock history, charting forty years of hits, including classics like "My Girl" and "The Way You Do the Things You Do." They've made fifty-nine albums and counting, and notched four Grammys. But tragedy has tracked the quintet: Of the five members of the classic lineup, only sixty-four-year-old baritone Otis Williams is still alive — and still a Temptation.

The Tempts hit it big at Motown in 1964. Eventually, Paul Williams, architect of the group's style and image, became unable to tour because of his alcoholism. He was released from the group in 1971 and continued drinking heavily. Two years later, the thirty-four-year-old was found dead in his car, not far from Motown's Detroit headquarters, of a self-inflicted gunshot wound to the head. Group mates Eddie Kendricks (a.k.a. Kendrick), David Ruffin, and Melvin Franklin were among the mourners at his funeral in Detroit's Tried Stone Baptist Church. Three decades on, the singer is still remembered. Recently, his plaque in Lincoln Memorial Park, near Detroit, bore fresh lipstick prints.

In the wee hours of June 1, 1991, a limousine dropped an ailing David Ruffin at a Pennsylvania hospital. An hour later, the gospel-trained Ruffin (born Davis Eli Ruffin), whose raspy growl had led the group, was dead of an accidental drug overdose that occurred in a Philadelphia crack house. Those

Melvin Franklin's resting place is in Hollywood.

who knew him were not surprised. Ruffin left the group in 1968 with several failed rehabs already behind him. He reunited with fellow alumnus Eddie Kendricks in the 1980s for a series of appearances and a couple of singles that did well, and he was working regularly at the time of his death. At Ruffin's funeral, fellow Motown graduate Stevie Wonder caught the mood of the 2,500 mourners when he sang "I Just Called to Say I Love You." The service was marred, however, when Kendricks was arrested for nonpayment of $26,000 in child support for the son he had with ex-wife Patricia.

With the soaring falsetto that topped tunes like "I Wish It Would Rain," Kendricks left the group in 1971 for a solo career that crested with disco before trickling down to oldies shows. Even after losing a lung to cancer – the result of thirty years of heavy smoking – Kendricks toured shortly before being hospitalized in 1991. At the time of his death, the fifty-two-year-old was suing Motown and his music publisher, claiming they had withheld royalties. After his funeral at the First Baptist Church, in Ensley, Alabama, he was laid to rest in Elwood Cemetery, in Birmingham.

For years, Melvin Franklin (born David Melvin English), whose ocean-deep bass anchored "Ain't Too Proud to Beg" and "Papa Was a Rollin' Stone," stepped through the Temptations' intricate dance moves in crippling pain from severe arthritis and diabetes. He retired in 1994, and the next year he was stricken with a brain seizure before dying at age fifty-two. He was laid to rest at Forest Lawn-Hollywood Hills. ✄

David Ruffin is buried in Woodlawn Cemetery in the group's hometown, Detroit.

ABOVE: *Paul Williams's grave is outside Detroit.*

OPPOSITE PAGE: *Eddie Kendricks's grave is in Alabama.*

fLoRence baLLaRD
June 30, 1943–February 22, 1976

maRy weLLs
May 13, 1943–July 26, 1992

Florence Ballard is buried in Detroit under her married name.

Motown Queens

*E*ven in death, Florence Ballard was upstaged by Diana Ross. As Ross entered Detroit's New Bethel Baptist Church to attend Ballard's funeral, she was booed by a crowd of thousands outside. Not surprising. The diva was often blamed for her sister Supreme's woes. Ballard formed and named the Supremes with neighbors Ross and Mary Wilson. As the trio rocketed up the charts, Motown impresario Berry Gordy felt Ross's higher-register voice and starlike presence would attract an even larger white audience. Ballard balked at calling the group Diana Ross and the Supremes, and in 1967, she was maneuvered out of the group with a token payment of $160,000. She later unsuccessfully sued Motown for unpaid royalties. Ballard eventually lost her fortune and her home, and for a time lived on welfare with her three children. In 1975, she received fifty thousand dollars from an unknown source; it may have been from Ross herself. It came too late. She died at age thirty-two of a heart attack, exacerbated by obesity and years of alcohol abuse.

Laid out in her powder blue choir robe, the singer was eulogized by the Reverend C.L. Franklin (Aretha's father), to two thousand-plus mourners, including Stevie Wonder and the Four Tops, who were pallbearers. When Franklin finished, Ross, who boldly sat in the front row reserved for family, jumped to her feet and asked for a microphone, stunning everyone. She persuaded an embarrassed Mary Wilson to join her in a private farewell to Ballard.

The mob outside overwhelmed the police line to grab at floral arrangements that were to be transported to Detroit Memorial Park. Attendants finally gave up, throwing the flowers into the crowd. Ross's limousine departed, and Ballard was laid to rest attended only by her family, Wilson, and the Four Tops. Her mother, Lurlee, said, "I think she died of a broken heart."

"The Queen of Motown," Mary Wells was called. Her 1964 hit "My Guy" was the label's first Number One song. With her husky, bluesy voice, she went on to notch more hits and even opened for the Beatles on a U.K. tour. She left Motown at age twenty-one and recorded for various labels but never regained her prominence. She kept up a busy touring schedule because, like many 1960s R&B performers, royalty rights were hard to secure. She eked out a modest living in Los Angeles with second husband Cecil Womack (brother of singer Bobby) and their four children. She and Womack divorced in 1977, and in 1990, Wells, a heavy smoker, was diagnosed with cancer of the larynx. Wells's choices: surgery, which would leave her virtually voiceless, or radiation, which would preserve some of her voice but might not kill the malignancy. She chose radiation, and because she had no health insurance or pension, the enormous bills left her destitute. The Rhythm & Blues Foundation, dedicated to helping the financially impacted pioneers of the music, came to the rescue, soliciting contributions from the likes of Frank Sinatra, Rod Stewart, Diana Ross, Michael Jackson, and the Temptations. The foundation also got Wells's union medical insurance reinstated. By the time she was laid to rest in Forest Lawn Memorial Park, the bills were paid. ✄

Mary Wells's grave is in Glendale, California.

Miles Davis

May 25, 1926–September 28, 1991

Volatile, arrogant, and charismatic, Miles Davis was a sonic explorer whose work extended beyond the boundaries of jazz; his 1969 album *Bitches Brew* and his concerts at the Fillmore theaters, in San Francisco and New York, powerfully affected rock. A collaboration with Jimi Hendrix was in the works at the time of the guitarist's death. Davis, who hated funerals, was persuaded by friends to go to Hendrix's service in Seattle, one of the few he ever attended.

Davis himself died at age sixty-five of pneumonia, respiratory failure, and stroke at St. John's Hospital and Health Center, in Santa Monica, California. At a memorial service at Manhattan's St. Peter's Lutheran Church, the Reverend Jesse Jackson said in his eulogy, "Sometimes by turning his back as he played a solitary song, he would let us hear him talking to God." Davis's headstone in New York City's Woodlawn Cemetery in the Bronx bears musical notes from his tune "Solar." In royal company, his resting place is only a few yards from that of Duke Ellington.

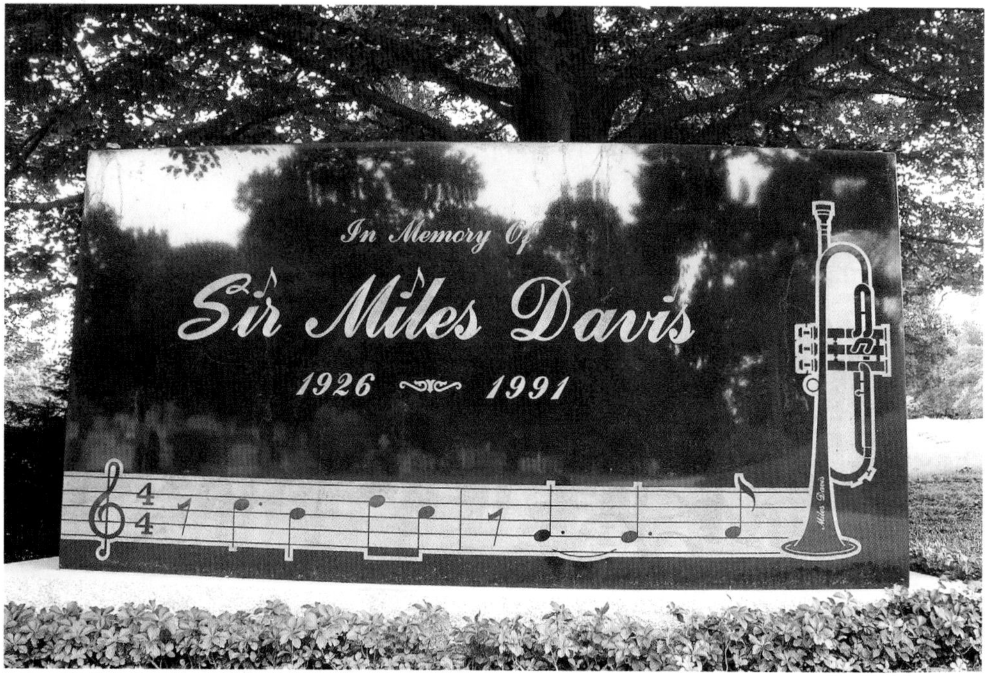

The trumpeter lies near the grave of Duke Ellington in the Bronx.

eric "eazy-e" wright
September 7, 1963–March 26, 1995

You might have expected that the end of Eric "Eazy-E" Wright would have come in a hail of bullets or over a mountain of drugs. With Ice Cube and Dr. Dre, the rapper-singer founded N.W.A (Niggaz With Attitude) in 1986. The group's double-platinum *Straight Outta Compton* brought gangsta rap into the mainstream, and the inflammatory and misogynistic *EFIL4ZAGGIN* reached Number One on the pop charts. Post-N.W.A, Wright continued running his Ruthless Records, allegedly started with money he made from dealing drugs, and predictably feuded with his ex–band mates. Surprisingly, though, he often went against the grain. He publicly sided with one of the policemen in the Rodney King case and attended a 1993 fund-raiser where President George Bush spoke.

His most unexpected turn came at age thirty-one, when he was diagnosed with AIDS, a disease mostly ignored in the macho rap community. From his bed at Los Angeles' Cedars-Sinai Medical Center, he urged homeboys to get tested. "I've learned in the last week that this thing is real and it doesn't discriminate," he said. "It affects everyone." His words hit home. In four days, the hospital received a record seven thousand calls about Wright's condition, and he received more cards and flowers than did Lucille Ball when she was hospitalized before her death in 1989. On his deathbed, Wright married Tomika Wood, the mother of one of his nine children by seven women. (Within months, however, his estate was besieged with lawsuits by business associates as well as potential heirs.)

A steady parade of cars booming Eazy-E raps cruised outside L.A.'s First African Methodist Episcopal Church during the funeral. In the chapel, some three thousand mourners listened to a eulogy by the Reverend Cecil Murray. "I know a little blackbird that sings," he said, pointing to the gold-colored, rose-draped coffin. "And his lyrics are, 'I want you to live. I want you to be careful. I want you to slow down.'" ✄

The N.W.A rapper is buried in Rose Hills Memorial Park, in Whittier, California.

99

"mother" maybelle carter
May 10, 1909–October 23. 1978

a.p. carter
December 15, 1891–November 7, 1960

sara carter
July 21, 1899–January 8, 1979

johnny cash
February 26, 1932–September 12, 2003

june carter cash
June 23, 1929–May 15, 2003

The Circle Is Unbroken

Behind the Mount Vernon Methodist Church in Maces Spring, Virginia, the modest headstones of A.P. and Sara Carter each carries a small replica of a gold record with the title WILL THE CIRCLE BE UNBROKEN? The answer has been a polyphonic yes. For almost eighty years, the intertwined kin of Carters and Cashes have been American music's first family. In 1927, mountaineers A.P. Carter, his wife Sara, and her cousin Maybelle harmonized on old-timey folk songs and gospel tunes, garnering a contract with Victor Records. Their recordings popularized the guitar as a folk instrument, and with standards including "Wabash Cannonball" and their million-selling "Wildwood Flower," the Carter Family became country's first superstar group.

Just as important, Maybelle's "Carter scratch" – flat-picking a melody while using her thumb to play rhythm on the bass strings – made her one of the most important guitar players in history. The style influenced artists ranging from Chet Atkins to Chuck Berry.

From the time Johnny Cash proposed to Maybelle's daughter June onstage in London in 1968, their biographies have been the stuff of pop-culture legend. She, the coauthor of her husband's hit "Ring of Fire" and his savior from drug addiction; he, a graduate of Sun Studio's "Million Dollar Quartet" (with Elvis Presley, Jerry Lee Lewis, and Carl Perkins) who transcended genres with a voice like nine miles of bad road. A member of both the Country Music and the Rock and Roll halls of fame, Cash duetted with Bob Dylan and later covered edgy songs by Beck, Soundgarden, and Nine Inch Nails, among others.

Married for thirty-five years, June and Johnny died less than five months apart – she of complications following valve-replacement surgery and he of diabetes-related health problems. Cash, already critically ill, attended her funeral in a wheelchair. The First Baptist Church of Hendersonville, Tennessee, was filled to its two thousand capacity with friends including Hank Williams Jr., Kris Kristofferson, and Trisha Yearwood. After performances by Sheryl Crow, Emmylou Harris, and the Oak Ridge Boys, Cash was wheeled next to June's light blue coffin for a private farewell.

The mourners at Cash's funeral, held in the same church, were a testament to his scope, embracing everyone from George Jones to Kid Rock. The Carter-Cash clan gathered at the altar near the end of the two-hour service, where the singer's coffin was surrounded by cotton, turnip, and corn plants like those that his sharecropper father cultivated. Said his sister Joanne Yates, "The Man in Black is wearing a white robe now."

Adjacent to Mother Maybelle's grave, Johnny Cash was laid to rest next to June in the family plot at Hendersonville Memorial Gardens. Along with flowers, guitar picks, and other mementos, visitors often leave quarters on Cash's stone. Cemetery officials are not sure why, but it may be a reference to Cash's version of the ballad of John Hardy, an outlaw who killed a man over twenty-five cents, then sought redemption before his own death. In ironic contrast to the ritual, hundreds of the couple's belongings, including boots, guitars, and even a Rolls-Royce and a pickup truck, were auctioned at Sotheby's, in accordance with Cash's will. So far, the couple's possessions have brought in more than four million dollars. ✄

Gold records are embossed on the headstones of A.P. and Sara Carter in southwestern Virginia.

Mother Maybelle and her husband, Ezra Carter, lie near daughter June and her husband Johnny Cash in Hendersonville, Tennessee.

carL perkins

April 9, 1932–January 19, 1998

Carl Perkins was astonished when George Harrison told him that he had learned guitar by fingering along with "Blue Suede Shoes." The 1956 rockabilly anthem that helped mold rock & roll was Sun Records' first million-seller. Though Perkins's solo career was plagued by bad breaks and personal problems, his songwriting lasted a lifetime. His tunes have charted for the Judds ("Let Me Tell You About Love") and his touring pal Johnny Cash ("Daddy Sang Bass"), among others. Perkins even helped produce Beatles recordings of his "Matchbox," "Honey Don't," and other songs.

It was fitting, then, that after the sixty-five-year-old's death from a series of strokes, Harrison sang an acoustic version of Perkins's "Your True Love" at his funeral in his hometown of Jackson, Tennessee. Inside the closed casket at R.E. Womack Memorial Chapel of Lambuth University, Perkins rested in his favorite gray pinstripe suit and a pair of blue suede shoes, and was surrounded by floral arrangements from Priscilla and Lisa Marie Presley, Bob Dylan, Elton John, Dolly Parton, and others. The 650 congregants – including Garth Brooks, former Sun label mate Jerry Lee Lewis, Sun founder Sam Phillips, Ricky Skaggs, and Johnny Rivers – heard eulogies by Wynonna Judd and Tennessee governor Don Sundquist. Before Perkins was interred in a mausoleum at Jackson's Ridgecrest Cemetery, Judd read a note sent by Dylan: "He really stood for freedom. That whole sound stood for all the degrees of freedom. It would just jump right off the turntable. We wanted to go where that was happening." We still do. ✄

George Harrison and Jerry Lee Lewis attended Perkins's funeral in Jackson, Tennessee.

WAYLON JENNINGS
June 15, 1937–February 13, 2002

He almost didn't live to become country's most wanted outlaw. As Buddy Holly's bass player in 1959, Waylon Jennings gave up his seat on a small plane to ailing fellow Texan J.P. "Big Bopper" Richardson. The chartered aircraft crashed moments after takeoff, killing Richardson, Holly, and Ritchie Valens. What he learned from Holly, Jennings said, was that music "shouldn't have any barriers to it." That's one reason he faced down what he called the "spangly suits" of Nashville tradition and took country in new directions by grabbing control of his recordings. Unlike the standard practice of the day, he chose the songs he wanted to record, cut them with his road band, and beefed up the drums. Over the course of his career, he recorded more than sixty albums, hit the C&W Top Ten fifty-three times, and sold forty million records. In 1976, the former DJ put together a compilation album called *Wanted: The Outlaws*, which included tracks by Jennings, his fourth and last wife Jessi Colter, Willie Nelson, and Tompall Glaser. It was the first platinum country album, followed the next year by *Ol' Waylon*, the first solo country compilation to go platinum. In the 1980s, he performed and recorded as part of the Highwaymen, a supergroup including Johnny Cash, Willie Nelson, and Kris Kristofferson. His rock credibility – thanks to songs like "Mammas Don't Let Your Babies Grow Up to Be Cowboys" – resulted in his being asked to perform several dates on the Lollapalooza Tour in 1996 with Metallica and Soundgarden.

But hard living on the road, some of it fueled by alcohol and a $1,500-per-day cocaine habit, took its toll. "I did more drugs than anybody you ever saw in your life," he once said. After becoming clean and sober, he mellowed. Well, a bit. When he was finally elected into the Country Music Hall of Fame, he snubbed the ceremony, sending one of his sons to accept. In his last years, the Grammy winner endured heart bypass surgery and, because of diabetes, had his foot amputated. *The Dukes of Hazzard* theme-song balladeer died quietly in his sleep at his Chandler, Arizona, home. Per his wishes, his funeral was a small, graveside ceremony in nearby Mesa, Arizona, attended by family and friends including Hank Williams Jr. and Travis Tritt. "Waylon Jennings was an American archetype," said Kristofferson. "The bad guy with a big heart." Indeed, the day after he died, the bouquet of Valentine roses he had ordered for Jessi arrived at their home. ✁

The veteran Outlaw died in his sleep at age sixty-three and is buried in Mesa, Arizona.

DOUG SAHM
November 6, 1941–November 18, 1999

Doug Sahm could play anything – and did. The San Antonio native was a master of styles from far beyond Lone Star State borders. As the Modish leader of a pseudo–British Invasion–style group, the Sir Douglas Quintet, he climbed the 1960s charts with "Mendocino" and "She's About a Mover." His eclecticism showed on his 1971 album, *The Return of Doug Saldana*, which featured Dr. John, Ray Charles's saxman David "Fathead" Newman, and conjunto accordionist Flaco Jimenez. As the founder of the Tejano supergroup the Texas Tornados, Sahm became – and remained – the godfather of the Tex-Mex sound.

The mayor of the Austin music scene died of a heart attack in a hotel room while vacationing in Taos, New Mexico. In mourning, Texans played his songs around the clock in Austin, and in San Antonio, more than a thousand fans, colleagues, and family members overflowed the Sunset Memorial Park Funeral Home for his service. Sahm was laid out in his black cowboy hat, purple jacket, and plenty of jewelry, his triple-neck Fender guitar resting nearby. After minister Sister Terry spoke, Sahm's drummer son Shandon offered a prayer, and his brother Shawn, also a musician, observed, "Nobody could do what my dad did. Thirty musicians couldn't do what my dad did." After Doug Sahm was interred beside his parents in a private ceremony at Sunset Memorial Park, the crowd adjourned to the Laboratory Brewing Company, where they raised a glass or three and jammed in memory of the most celestial of cosmic cowboys. Since his death, a Doug Sahm tribute is held annually in either Austin or San Antonio. ✄

The leader of the Sir Douglas Quintet was laid out in a purple jacket and cowboy hat, then buried in San Antonio, Texas.

RUFUS THOMAS

March 26, 1917–December 15, 2001

I'm young and loose and full of juice. I got the goose, so what's the use?" That's how the ebullient Rufus Thomas kicked off his radio show in the forties on WDIA, the first radio station in the South to feature black DJs. And when the share-cropper's son died at eighty-four, he was still the loosest goose in Memphis. He had credentials, charisma . . . and chops. His strutting "Bear Cat," a comic answer song to Big Mama Thornton's "Hound Dog," was Sun Records' first national hit, in 1953, and he charted again in the sixties and seventies with novelty tunes "Walking the Dog"

and "Do the Funky Chicken." He sometimes complained that Sun owner Sam Phillips was just waiting for a "white boy to sing our music," but Thomas was colorblind on the air and played Elvis along with Junior Parker. Outlandish in knee-high gold boots and brightly colored shorts, the self-described "world's oldest teenager" became a founding performer at Stax Records, where his daughter Carla Thomas teamed with Otis Redding on soul duets. Early on, Thomas mounted Memphis talent shows that introduced future stars including Bobby "Blue" Bland, Ike Turner, and B.B. King. "He was a mentor to me," said King to the 2,500 mourners attending Thomas's funeral at the Mississippi Boulevard Christian Church, "and to be honest with you, one of the greatest entertainers I ever met."

The showman was played offstage in true Memphis style. His hearse, preceded by a brass band playing "Just a Closer Walk With Thee," was driven in a motorcade down Beale Street. His grave in a rural churchyard miles from downtown is modest. But his memorial marker at the intersection of Beale Street and Rufus Thomas Boulevard (naturally) presents a proper remembrance. It reads:

RUFUS THOMAS
AMBASSADOR OF SOUL
THE KING OF RHYTHM & BLUES
OUT SPOKEN AND OUTTA SIGHT. . . . ✄

The flamboyant master of Memphis soul has a modest grave in rural Tennessee.

JESSIE HILL
December 9, 1932–September 17, 1996

The perpetrator of "Ooh Poo Pah Doo" has a plywood marker in a New Orleans paupers cemetery.

Jessie Hill had only one hit, and he played the hell out of it. His 1960 party classic "Ooh Poo Pah Doo" sold 800,000 copies and has been covered more than a hundred times. One of New Orleans' indelible characters, Hill played drums for Professor Longhair, worked with Dr. John, and sang on his own when he could get a gig. He heard "Ooh Poo Pah Doo" in a joint called Shy Guy's, sung by a man known only as Big Four, who sometimes performed for drinks. Scribbling the lyrics on a paper sack, Hill used it as a gimmick in his lounge act. To his surprise, the tune became a Mardi Gras favorite and then moved up the national charts. Hill wrote prolifically and recorded some afterward but never scored big again. When his "Ooh Poo Pah Doo" royalties ran out, he got a taxi license, bought a black Cadillac, and dubbed it the Poo Cab. By the late 1980s, however, he had slipped into alcohol and drug addiction, lost his cab driver's license to DWI convictions, and was nearly penniless.

After his death from heart and kidney failure, the New Orleans music community came to the rescue. Funeral expenses were partially paid by Dr. John. Antoinette K-Doe, wife of Ernie K-Doe, made a suit for Hill to wear at his wake, so, she said, he would look like "an emperor on his way to heaven." A brass band accompanied the hearse to Holt Cemetery, a city-owned plot for paupers. On the hot and humid morning at the graveside service, the perspiring minister said, "Okay, let's get this nigger in the ground and go home." Hill lies under a plywood marker, which sometimes topples over. He does get visitors, although the mementos they leave are achingly modest. On a recent day, the sparse grass was decorated with two unsmoked cigarettes and two empty cans of Bud Light. ✁

BESSIE SMITH
April 15, 1894–September 26, 1937

JANIS JOPLIN
January 19, 1943–October 4, 1970

When the 1920s roared, Bessie Smith was one of the highest-paid black performers in the world. But the Empress of the Blues endured the hard times she sang about when the Depression nearly destroyed the music business. In 1937, just as her career was picking up steam again, Smith suffered horrific injuries in a Mississippi Delta car crash. At age forty-three, she died of massive blood loss at an infirmary for blacks in nearby Clarksdale. Her producer John Hammond later set off a racial firestorm when he told *Downbeat* magazine that Smith might have lived had she not been refused admittance to a white hospital. The story was proven false, but as late as 1960, Edward Albee echoed the myth in his play *The Death of Bessie Smith*.

Even without the fable, her end had a tragic poignancy. Mobbed by mourners, Smith's memorial service was moved from a Philadelphia funeral home to the O.V. Catto Elks Lodge, where ten thousand people filed past her gold-trimmed coffin. Despite the pomp, the singer's grave in Sharon Hill, Pennsylvania, went unmarked until 1970, when a letter to the editor of the *Philadelphia Inquirer* pointing out the fact attracted the attention of Janis Joplin, the Texas-born blues queen then riding her own wave of fame. The hard-living Joplin, who called Smith "my early idol," and NAACP official Juanita Green, a former Smith employee, bought Smith an elegant headstone.

Two months later, Joplin died of a heroin overdose in a Los Angeles motel room at age twenty-seven. The Texas-born rebel was cremated, and her ashes were scattered in the Pacific. ✥

Janis Joplin bought the headstone for Smith's unmarked grave just months before her own death.

JOHN Lee HOOKER
August 22, 1917–June 21, 2001

"When I'm gone, I don't want any weeping, crying, falling around, gnashing of teeth," John Lee Hooker told his daughter Zakiya not long before he died. "I want people to be joyous, because I'm going home. I'm tired. I've made a journey." Some journey. Since his 1949 single "Boogie Chillen," which sold a million copies, Hooker became a major connection between urban, electric blues and rock & roll. By his estimate, he made over a hundred albums, and his influence on everyone from the Stones to Springsteen to Santana was indelible. Miles Davis, with whom Hooker worked on a movie soundtrack, called him "the funkiest man alive, buried up to [his] neck in mud."

Some 1,800 mourners attended the bluesman's funeral at Oakland Interstake Center Auditorium, not far from his home in Los Altos, California. Peers Buddy Guy, Ry Cooder, and more than twenty former members of Hooker's band filed by the highly polished mahogany casket, flanked by an oversize guitar made of red and black carnations. Bonnie Raitt, a friend of thirty years who shared a 1990 Grammy with Hooker for their duet, "I'm in the Mood," recalled to the audience, "I had never heard anything coming out of any man that was as scary and evocative and as intoxicating. And I feel the same way about him today."

Hooker was interred in the Garden of Ages mausoleum at Oakland's magnificently landscaped Chapel of the Chimes. The cemetery, with its terraced gardens, boasts rolling skylights and is the first to have electrically operated roofs. The musician would have gotten a kick out of that fact. As his oldest daughter, Francis C. McBee, said in an open letter to her father at his funeral, "You did things your way. Instead of dying during the day, you died during the night so that you could have a clean getaway. Instead of leaving by the front door, you stepped out the back door and went quietly into history." ✄

"I want people to be joyous, because I'm going home," the bluesman once said of death.

HOWLIN' WOLf
June 10, 1910–January 10, 1976

MUDDY WATERS
April 4, 1915–April 30, 1983

WILLIE DIXON
July 1, 1915–January 29, 1992

Sweet Home Chicago

*T*hree men from the Delta carried their music to Chicago, where they forged indelible links to rock & roll. For much of their careers, they recorded for Chess Records, the Chicago crèche of urban blues. All three are buried in their adopted hometown.

With a strangled growl, a mouth-harp riff, and hard-driving numbers like "Smokestack Lightnin' " and "Killing Floor," Howlin' Wolf (born Chester Arthur Burnett) brought Mississippi to Michigan Avenue. From there, the signature sounds of the six-foot-two, three-hundred-pound singer flowed through rock, covered by the Grateful Dead, the Rolling Stones, and the Doors, among others. Wolf kept a relentless performing schedule, but kidney disease finally slowed his pace. He died at the Hines

Veterans Administration Hospital in Chicago at age sixty-five. Three decades after his internment at Oak Ridge Cemetery, fans still decorate his grave with gifts of guitar picks and coins.

The man with the mojo, Muddy Waters (born McKinley Morganfield) electrified the blues – and audiences. His 1948 "Rollin' Stone" was a "race record" hit; by the 1960s, it had furnished names for a supergroup and a magazine. His distinctive sound – "Hoochie Coochie Man," "I Just Want to Make Love to You" – defined Chicago blues. He died of a heart attack in his sleep at his suburban Westmont, Illinois, home at age sixty-eight. His grave in Chicago's Restvale Cemetery is close to that of blues harmonica great "Big Walter" Horton.

The hundreds of songs penned by bassist Willie Dixon comprise a core playlist of rock: "Little Red Rooster," "Bring It On Home," "Spoonful," "My Babe," and dozens more. At Chess, the onetime–Golden Gloves boxer ran the label's house band and oversaw the production of dozens of classics. His vision, however, went far beyond the studio. With the royalties from a successful copyright battle with Led Zeppelin over the song "Whole Lotta Love," Dixon established the charitable Blues Heaven Foundation, dedicated to the education and preservation of the blues. Following his death from complications due to diabetes, Dixon was interred at Burr Oak Cemetery, the Chicago area's first African-American cemetery, whose residents include civil rights martyr Emmett Till and musicians Dinah Washington and Otis Spann. A year later, Dixon's foundation bought the long-abandoned Chess studio, saving it from destruction. ✄

The Wolf is buried near Chicago, in Hillside, Illinois.

ABOVE: *Dixon is buried near Dinah Washington outside Chicago in Alsip, Illinois.*

OPPOSITE PAGE: *Like Wolf, Waters's birth name, Morganfield, is on his stone.*

JOHN BeLUSHI
January 24, 1949–March 5, 1982

Wouldn't you know it? Even after his exit from "acute cocaine and heroin intoxication," as his death certificate has it, Blues Brother "Joliet" Jake still stole the show. For starters, his casket wouldn't fit in the little seven-seat Warner Bros. corporate jet that flew his body from Los Angeles to the tony Massachusetts island of Martha's Vineyard, where he and his wife, Judy, had a home. So his remains, accompanied by his longtime agent Bernie Brillstein, were placed in a body bag and strapped into one of the plane's seats.

Following the funeral at the West Tisbury Congregational Church, Belushi's closest pal and Vineyard neighbor Dan Aykroyd led the cortege to Abel's Hill Cemetery on his Harley, wearing black jeans and a leather motorcycle jacket. He loudly gunned the engine, some said, so that John might hear it, wherever he was. Snow was falling at the graveside when James Taylor sang "That Lonesome Road."

Belushi once said he wanted a Viking funeral, his body set on fire and sent out to sea. Aykroyd told author David Michaelis, who wrote about the pair's friendship in *The Best of Friends: Profiles of Extraordinary Friendship*, "Well, *that* would have been a circus. There would have been a flotilla of press boats, and what if the fire had gone out too soon. . . ." Aykroyd said that he murmured to his departed pal, "The Viking funeral is out. Just relax. We're putting you here in Abel's Hill with the whalers and the Indians and the pirates and the smugglers. You'll be fine. There are so many ghosts on this island. Good bones here, man."

Two days later, a thousand mourners at Manhattan's Cathedral of St. John the Divine (get it?)

were stunned when Aykroyd, instead of eulogizing his pal, pulled a boombox from his backpack and blasted "The Two Thousand Pound Bee," an obscure dance instrumental by the Ventures. The two *Saturday Night Live* "Killer Bee" alums had heard the tune on the radio and vowed that after one of them died, the other would play the song at his funeral.

Show over? Not by a long shot. Belushi ended up with three headstones in two graveyards, and he may not be buried beneath any of them. As do many celebrity resting places, the comedian's grave, near that of famously cantankerous playwright Lillian Hellman, became a magnet for fans and oddballs, who deposited the usual sacrifices and offerings and, according to the cemetery, caused "tourist damage." At some point, Belushi was reburied near the Abel's Hill entrance, beneath a piratical skull and crossbones, with the declaration, I MAY BE GONE, BUT ROCK AND ROLL LIVES ON.

The whereabouts of his body soon became fodder for Internet news-group threads. Some insist that the body may not be under the second headstone either (the first is still in place), and, to deter any attempts to unearth it, the coffin was actually buried in an unmarked location. And then there's the odd fact that on the hometown family cenotaph in Chicago's Elmwood Memorial Cemetery, Belushi's name is listed with those of his parents. So where's Johnny? Only his wife and a few intimates know for sure. In the summer of '82, actor/pal Treat Williams stopped by Abel's Hill and was struck by a sign left by a fan: HE COULD HAVE GIVEN US A LOT MORE LAUGHS BUT NOOOO . . . ✄

Here Lies Buried
The Body Of
JOHN BELUSHI

JANUARY 24, 1949
MARCH 5, 1982

I may be gone, but
Rock and Roll lives on.

The third of Belushi's graves, near the entrance to Abel's Hill Cemetery in Martha's Vineyard

IN LOVING MEMORY OF
1949   OUR SON   1982
JOHN A. BELUSHI
"HE GAVE US LAUGHTER"

BELUSHI

FATHER
ADAM
JAN. 2, 1918 – MAY 30, 1996

MOTHER
AGNES
MAR. 23, 1922 – DEC. 21, 1989

ABOVE: *The family plot in Chicago*

OPPOSITE PAGE: *The other Martha's Vineyard grave*

MC5

rob tyner

November 12, 1944–September 18, 1991

fred "sonic" smith

September 13, 1949–November 3, 1994

THIS PAGE: *Frontman Tyner's headstone bears both his stage and birth names.*

OPPOSITE PAGE: *Smith's marker is a stone from Scotland.*

MC5 never hit the charts, yet it was the revolutionary heart of the 1960s. So it is sadly appropriate that two members of the groundbreaking quintet died of heart failure, both in middle age. The ear-splitting Detroit house band of underground poet John Sinclair's White Panther Party once described its act as the James Brown Revue on Acid. Committed to social rebellion, MC5 (Motor City Five) entered rock legend with its lyrics "Kick Out the Jams, Motherfuckers" and with its righteous performance during the riot-torn 1968 Democratic National Convention in Chicago. But after three albums in four years, MC5 dissolved. Frontman Rob Tyner (born Robert Derminer), who took his stage name from John Coltrane's pianist McCoy Tyner, found some success as a songwriter and photographer before he suffered a heart attack at age forty-six while returning to his Detroit home from a supermarket. His wife, Becky, and daughter, Elizabeth, attended the brief ceremony at his grave in Roseland Park Cemetery in the nearby suburb of Berkley.

Post-MC5, lead guitarist Fred "Sonic" Smith married poet and musician Patti Smith in 1980 and settled in the Motor City suburb of St. Clair

Shores, with their two children. He formed several groups with other area musicians, and in 1988 produced and played on his wife's album *Dream of Life*. Taken ill at home with liver disease, he died a few days later at St. John Hospital. His grave in Detroit's Elmwood Cemetery is marked by a tall stone brought from the Scottish Highlands, where he and his wife went hiking. Patti Smith created a memorial fund in her husband's name. The beneficiary is Detroit's Old Mariner's Church, where the couple was married. And she remembered the guitarist in her song "Dead to the World": "The life in his fingers unwound my existence." ✄

The New York Dolls

BILLY MURCIA
1951–1972

JOHNNY THUNDERS
July 15, 1952–April 23, 1991

ARTHUR KANE
1949–July 13, 2004

JERRY NOLAN
May 7, 1946–January 14, 1992

"You can't put your arms around a memory," Johnny Thunders sang. Maybe so, but it's hard not to embrace Thunders (born John Anthony Genzale) and the rest of the New York Dolls. In the early 1970s, the quartet set the stage for punk rock with a frantic blur of unkempt cross-dressing and calculated amateurishness. Despite the platform shoes and mascara, their two albums – and their attitudes – were down-to-earth. Filmmaker and friend Rachel Amodeo once attended Thanksgiving dinner with Thunders's family. "It was typical Queens Italian," she said. "The parish priest even showed up. And before Johnny left, they all told him he was too thin and gave him a lot of leftovers."

Johnny Thunders's grave in Mount St. Mary's Cemetery

But the rock & roll lifestyle took a toll that concern couldn't counteract. The Dolls' original drummer, Billy Murcia, suffocated to death at twenty-one after washing down pills with whiskey on a 1972 English tour. (His burial place is unknown.) Amazingly, Thunders, one of the downtown scene's most notorious drug users, made it to age thirty-eight before dying of a heroin overdose in a New Orleans hotel room. Aerosmith's Steven Tyler, among others, came to the two-day wake at a Queens, New York, funeral home. Alvin Eng, a fan who attended Thunders's funeral, remembered, "On the right aisle you had all of the bridge-and-tunnel punks (myself included) who were there to mourn Johnny Thunders. But on the other side of the aisle were the mourners of John Anthony Genzale. . . . [They] had these dark shadows around their dark, Italian immigrant eyes."

In a cold drizzle, graveside at Mount St. Mary's Cemetery in Queens, Jerry Nolan, who had replaced Murcia on drums, said, "Today I'm the most lonely guy in the world." Less than a year later, Nolan, who had undergone treatment for pneumonia and meningitis brought on by substance abuse, himself died of a stroke at age forty-five. He also rests in Mount St. Mary's. Dolls bassist Arthur "Killer" Kane survived a drinking problem and being stabbed by a girlfriend who did not want him to go on tour, to die at age fifty-five of leukemia. His death came just weeks after a successful London reunion gig with Dolls singer David Johansen and guitarist Sylvain Sylvain. A devout Mormon, Kane worked before his death at a church genealogy center in Los Angeles; a memorial service was held for him at the Church of the Latter Day Saints temple there. But at this writing, the disposition of his remains is unknown. ✄

Jerry Nolan's plot, in Queens, New York, not far from Thunders's resting place

RONNIE van zant
January 15, 1949–October 20, 1977

steve gaines
September 9, 1949–October 20, 1977

cassie gaines
January 9, 1948–October 20, 1977

Leon wilkeson
April 2, 1952–July 27, 2001

allen collins
July 19, 1952–January 23, 1990

OPPOSITE PAGE: *Van Zant's body was moved to a crypt after his original grave was disturbed.*

Lynyrd Skynyrd

The most successful Southern rock outfit was also one of the most star-crossed. Just three days after Lynyrd Skynyrd's sixth album, *Street Survivors*, was released, the band boarded its chartered Convair 240 – the same plane used by John F. Kennedy in his 1960 campaign – in Greenville, South Carolina. The Jacksonville-based group was headed for Baton Rouge when the two-engine craft plunged into a swamp near Gillsburg, Mississippi, killing six of the twenty-six aboard. Along with crew members and road manager Dean Kilpatrick, Skynyrd founder and frontman Ronnie Van Zant, new guitarist Steve Gaines, and his sister Cassie Gaines, a backup singer, also died. The three musicians were all twenty-eight years old. Fuel shortage was a probable cause for the accident, but a lawsuit later faulted the pilots and the plane itself. The *Survivors* album cover, depicting the band standing in flames, was quickly pulled and replaced with a new design.

Van Zant's tomb bears a personal message from his family.

124

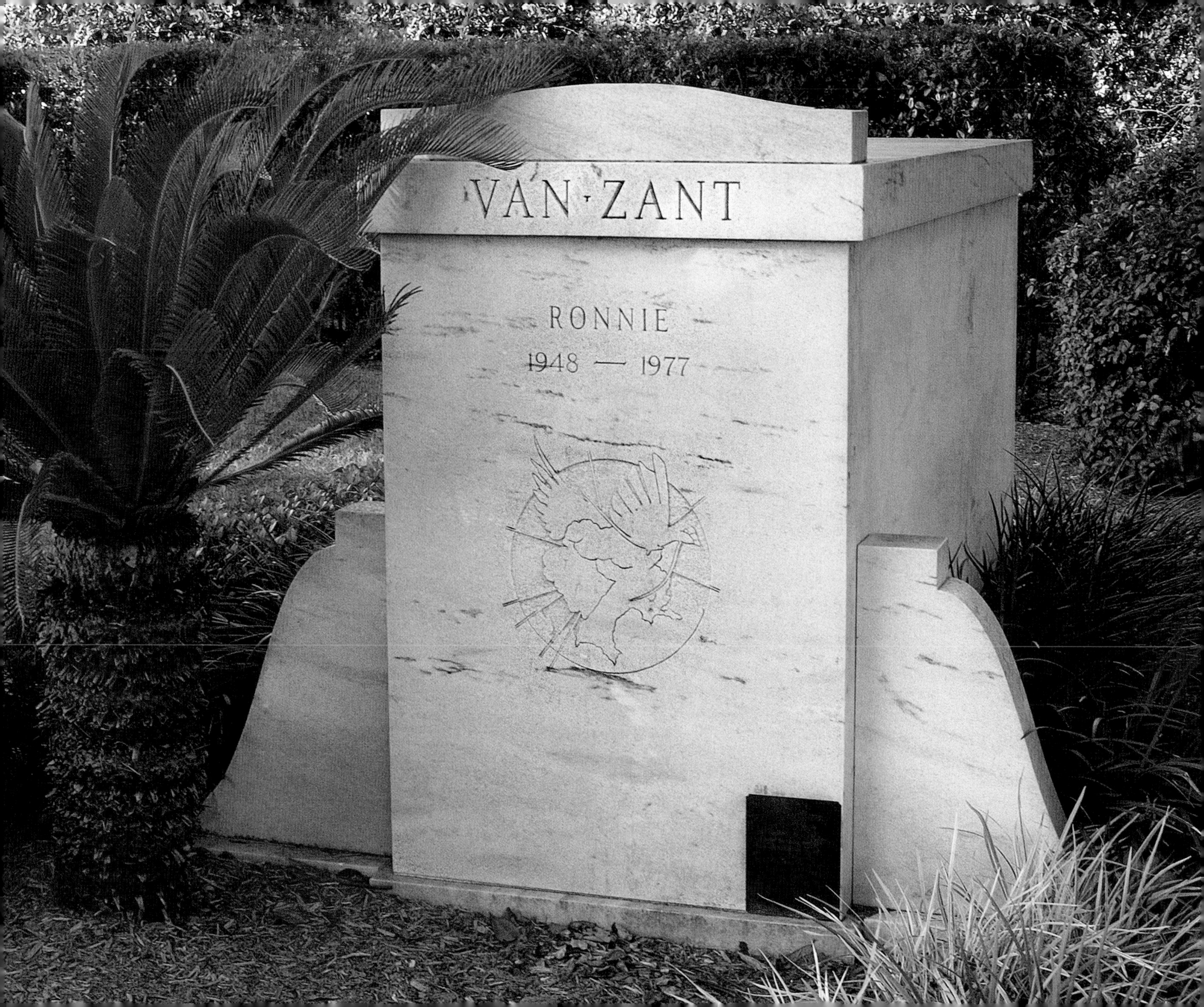
VAN·ZANT
RONNIE
1948 — 1977

A BRIEF CANDLE · BOTH ENDS BURNING
AN ENDLESS MILE, A BUS WHEEL TURNING
A FRIEND TO SHARE A LONESOME TIME
A HANDSHAKE AND A SIP OF WINE
SAY IT LOUD AND LET IT RING
THAT WE'RE ALL PART OF EVERYTHING
THE FUTURE, PRESENT AND THE PAST
FLY ON PROUD BIRD, YOU'RE FREE AT LAST.
C. DANIELS

These words by fiddler Charlie Daniels adorn a bench next to Van Zant's grave.

Wilkeson's plot collects Skynyrdesque offerings.

Cassie and Steve Gaines were cremated and memorialized in their hometown, Miami, Oklahoma, before their ashes were buried beside Van Zant's grave in Jacksonville Memory Gardens, in suburban Orange Park, Florida. The singer was laid to rest there after a funeral at which Charlie Daniels and the band .38 Special sang "Amazing Grace," a Van Zant favorite. "Free Bird," the Skynyrd hit written as a tribute to the late Duane Allman, soon became a fitting anthem for the band's own losses.

The heartbreak just kept on coming. The graves quickly became an attraction for local teens as well as Skynyrd fans from all over. Visitors behaved themselves, doing little damage to the markers or the grounds, until 1982, when the three-hundred-pound marble bench beside Van Zant's resting place was stolen. It was soon recovered by the police. Things turned more gruesome in 2000. At 3:00 a.m. on a June morning, police discovered that Van Zant's above-ground marble memorial had been smashed and his casket dragged out. The plastic bag containing Steve Gaines's ashes also had been removed from its metal urn and torn open. Ronnie's widow,

Judy Van Zant Jenness, and the couple's daughter, Melody Van Zant, were horrified. "They just couldn't believe anyone would do anything like this," said Aaron Webb, manager of the Freebird Café, which was owned by the women. A wall was erected around the site, but to little avail. Two weeks later, a man was arrested while trying to kick down the barrier. Judy then had all three bodies moved to an undisclosed location but told fans they could continue to visit the original gravesites, which were left intact.

Misfortune also befell Skynyrd members who survived the plane crash. In 1986, guitarist Allen Collins smashed his car in an accident near his Jacksonville home, killing his girlfriend and leaving him permanently paralyzed from the waist down. He later pled no contest to drunk driving and manslaughter charges. Due to his injuries, he was unable to play during the next Skynyrd tour. But, as stipulated by his court sentence, Collins made appearances onstage to warn kids about drunk driving. His disability left him with decreased lung capacity, and in 1989 he contracted pneumonia. He died the next year and was interred at Jacksonville's River-

Steve Gaines's ashes were moved to an undisclosed location after this urn was raided.

His sister Cassie's resting place has a concrete bench.

side Memorial Park Cemetery, next to his wife Kathy, who had died a decade earlier of complications during pregnancy.

In 2001, hard-drinking Skynyrd bassist Leon Wilkeson died of liver disease at age forty-nine and was buried near Collins. Wilkeson had carried a Bible wherever he went, said the pastor at his funeral, because "You can be a rock & roller and still love the Lord." Four decades after their founding, Lynyrd Skynyrd still tours, with Ronnie's brother Johnny on vocals. And, according to the trade magazine *Death Care Business Advisor*, "Free Bird" has become one of the most requested songs to be played during funerals. ✄

tommy caLDweLL
November 9, 1949–April 28, 1980

toy caLDweLL
November 13, 1947–February 25, 1993

The Marshall
Tucker Band

Tommy was killed in a car crash.

*I*t was the most heartbreaking damn thing I've ever seen," recalled Capricorn Records founder Phil Walden. "There was old Toy Caldwell Sr., just as plain as country dirt, sitting by the coffin of his boy. He was burying his third son. He looked so forlorn." The fate of the Caldwell boys of Spartanburg, South Carolina, could have come out of Faulkner. Guitarist/songwriter Toy and bassist Tommy Caldwell cofounded the Marshall Tucker Band, which loped through the 1970s with a distinctive mix of Southern rock, country, pop, and even a jazz lick or two. They recorded two platinum and seven gold albums, and such hits as "Heard It in a Love Song," and even played at President Jimmy Carter's inauguration. But on April 22, 1980, Tommy's car flipped over in a collision, and he died of his injuries six days later at Spartanburg General Hospital. His death came just a month after Tim, the youngest of the three Caldwell brothers, was killed in an auto accident.

The band, named after the piano tuner who owned its rehearsal hall, soldiered on, but by 1983, Toy and the two other members sold their interest in the group. Toy struggled to overcome a drug problem and build a solo career. He issued an eponymous album in 1992. A year later, his body was found by his wife Abbie in their Moore, South Carolina, home; he died of respiratory failure. "He called me on the day he died," Walden recalled. "One of the best songwriters in the South, and he was broke. He wanted to borrow money to rent studio time to record some new songs." The Vietnam veteran was laid to rest near Tommy in Spartanburg's Floyd Greenlawn Cemetery. ✄

I LOVE YOU NOW AND FOREVER
"AB"
TOY T. CALDWELL JR.
LOVING FATHER OF CASSADY AND GENEAL
NOV. 13, 1947   FEB. 25, 1993

Toy died of respiratory failure.

Lisa "Lefteye" Lopes
May 27, 1971–April 25, 2002

No one is sure why visitors leave coins on the TLC singer's likeness.

Since it topped the charts in 1995, TLC's inspirational anthem "Waterfalls" is often requested at the funerals of those who have died young. So it was fitting that some of its lyrics were inscribed on Lisa "Lefteye" Lopes's white casket: "Dreams are hopeless aspirations, in hopes of coming true, believe in yourself . . . the rest is up to me and you."

On May 2, 2002, ten thousand mourners crowded into the New Birth Missionary Baptist Church in Lithonia, Georgia, to lay a dream to rest. Several thousand more stood outside, listening to the service on loudspeakers. Lopes died when the SUV she was driving flipped over in Honduras, where she was vacationing. Janet Jackson, Whitney Houston, and Bobby Brown joined surviving TLC members Tionne "T-Boz" Watkins and Rozonda "Chilli" Thomas, family, and friends for the music-filled ceremony.

Lopes's grave in nearby Hillandale Memorial Gardens is covered with a bronze slab designed by her mother, Wanda Lopes-Coleman. But she hasn't been to the cemetery in over a year. "It's too hard for me," she said. A dozen or so people a week make the trip, including musicians. Both the famous and the ordinary leave coins on top of a sculpted image of the singer. "We have no idea why," said a cemetery spokeswoman. "We don't move the money. Sometimes it's gone, sometimes it stays."

One regular caller is former Atlanta Falcons star Andre Rison. When Lopes was stormily dating Rison in 1994, she started a fire that burned down his mansion. "She was my heart," Rison said after her funeral. "We're going to let her fly with wings, like angels do. She's truly and definitely an angel." ✄

Lisa
Nicole
Lopes
"Lefteye"
May 27, 1971
April 25, 2002

frankie Lymon

September 30, 1942–February 27, 1968

IN LOVING MEMORY
OF MY HUSBAND

FRANK J.
LYMON

SEPT. 30, 1942 – FEB. 27, 1968

Only twenty-five when he died, Lymon is buried in the Bronx.

By the time he was eighteen, Frankie Lymon's career was effectively over. Five years earlier, he and his group the Teenagers had laid down the endurable "Why Do Fools Fall in Love?" The cherubic Lymon was the first black teen idol, but by age fifteen, he had quit the Teenagers for a drab solo career, fueled by an increasing dependence on heroin. In 1968, he played his last gig in his home-town of New York City, then a few days later he was found dead in the bathroom of his grand-mother's apartment, an empty syringe by his side. His widow, schoolteacher Emira Eagle, erected a headstone in St. Raymond's Cemetery in the Bronx.

Lymon's end was the beginning of a lengthy and bitter fight over millions of dollars in "Fools" royal-ties. The song, covered endlessly, was a hit for Diana Ross and was featured on the *American Graffiti* soundtrack. Emira's bid to renew her husband's copyright was challenged by record executive Morris Levy, who had bought the catalogue of the song's original label, Gee, and had listed himself as coauthor of the song with Lymon. To discredit Emira, Levy found two women who claimed that they were also married to the singer. After more lawsuits and appeals, Emira won the case. But two of the Teenagers, Jimmy Merchant and Herman Santiago, sued to be named the song's rightful authors. In 1992, they won their bid, but the decision was later reversed on appeal. The 1998 biopic, *Why Do Fools Fall in Love*, which presented the story through the eyes of Emira and the two other women, occasioned more squabbling, and Santiago publicly questioned the accuracy of the film. The authorship battle even made it into the first season of *The Sopranos*. The series' scene-stealing music mogul, Hesh, was mod-eled on Levy. ✄

BOBBY FuLLeR
October 22, 1943–July 18, 1966

Bobby Fuller had one very big hit and one very mysterious death. The native Texan soared into the Top Ten in 1966 with "I Fought the Law." Along with its teen-rebel attitude, the tune, penned by Sonny Curtis, a member of Buddy Holly's Crickets, caught the mood of the civil rights movement. It had staying power, too, and has been covered by dozens of groups, including the Clash and the Dead Kennedys. Fuller racked up a couple more hits, allowing him to live large on the Sunset Strip before his life ended in bizarre circumstances.

The twenty-two-year-old was found dead in his mother's Oldsmobile, near the apartment he shared with his brother and band mate Randy Fuller. His body was soaked in gasoline. A fuel can and a book of matches were found next to him. The death was ruled a suicide, which left those who knew Fuller incredulous. He hadn't been depressed, they said. Plus, some facts pointed to murder: No car keys were found at the scene, and what about the bruises on his chest mentioned in the police report? Rumors circulated that he had been experimenting with LSD; that he was dating a mobbed-up club owner's girlfriend; that a payola deal had gone belly-up. Three months after the singer was buried at Forest Lawn-Hollywood Hills cemetery, the coroner's ruling was changed to accidental death by asphyxiation from inhaling gasoline fumes but still maintained that there was no evidence of foul play. By then, Bob Keane, president of Del-Fi Records, Fuller's label, had hired a private investigator to look into the case. He quit after a few days, however, claiming he had been shot at by a would-be assassin. Thirty years after Fuller's demise, TV's *Unsolved Mysteries* revisited the events but drew no new conclusion. ✄

Unsolved Mysteries *documented the musician's demise.*

ernie k-doe

February 22, 1936–July 5, 2001

The "Mother-in-Law" singer was given a two-hour funeral, a New Orleans parade, and a smashing plaque.

ERNIE K-DOE (1936-2001)

"AFTER ME, THERE WILL BE NO OTHER…"

EMPEROR OF THE UNIVERSE AND FRIENDS OF NEW ORLEANS CEMETERIES GRAND MARSHALL ERNIE K-DOE WAS BURIED IN THIS TOMB ON JULY 13, 2001. ALONG WITH THE "STAR SPANGLED BANNER", HIS SIGNATURE R&B CLASSIC "MOTHER IN LAW" WILL BE ONE OF ONLY TWO SONGS TO ULTIMATELY BE REMEMBERED. HIS WAKE AND FUNERAL COMPRISED THE MOST SPECTACULAR SEND-OFF NEW ORLEANS HAS EVER EXPERIENCED. TOMB OWNER HEATHER TWICHELL OF THE DUVAL FAMILY GRACIOUSLY DONATED THE BURIAL SPACE.

FRIENDS OF NEW ORLEANS CEMETERIES, 2001
WWW.FONOC.ORG

How does a one-hit wonder meet eternity? Forgotten and unmourned? Not Ernie K-Doe, the irrepressible perpetrator of the 1961 novelty tune "Mother-in-Law." After a couple of moderate hits, K-Doe (Kador by birth), the son of a New Orleans preacher, slipped from the pop charts and into two decades of indigent alcoholism, sometimes singing for change on French Quarter streets. But in the mid-nineties he met and married helpmate Antoinette Fox and cleaned up his act to become a legend in local charity work. He and Antoinette also opened Ernie K-Doe's Mother-in-Law Lounge, a classic New Orleans juke joint that became a gathering place for musicians and R&B fans. Grandly presiding in a pink tuxedo, K-Doe, the self-crowned "Emperor of the World," told visitors, including the likes of Little Richard and Eric Clapton, that only three songs would last forever: "Amazing Grace," "The Star-Spangled Banner," and "Mother-in-Law," because, he said, "as long as there are people on earth, there will always be mother-in-laws."

His send-off did not begin well. After he died, at age sixty-five, the hospital temporarily lost his body. Worse, he had no burial plot. In the Big Easy, internments must be aboveground because of the high water table. And cemetery space is so limited that tombs are handed down through generations. To the rescue: historical preservationist Anna Ross Twichell. "I knew Ernie because he was active in the Friends of New Orleans Cemeteries, our group that works to restore and preserve graveyards," she said. "My daughter Heather inherited the Duval family tomb from her father, my ex-husband, in St. Louis #2, one of the oldest cemeteries. She's a musician too. A classical harpist; can you believe it? And she offered Antoinette a place for Ernie."

More than five thousand people paid their respects at the wake in historic Gallier Hall, where Jefferson Davis and General Beauregard had once lain in state. K-Doe, the king of Krewe du Vieux, a venerable Mardi Gras club, was decked out in his crown, sash, and white tuxedo. He lay in a casket custom-built to fit beneath the low curved roof of the Duval tomb's top shelf. After R&B singer Irma Thomas performed "No Not One," Jean Knight sang her hit, "Mr. Big Stuff," and K-Doe's backup band, the Blue Eyed Soul Revue, ripped it up as mourners danced in the aisles.

Following a two-hour funeral, the procession to St. Louis #2 featured the Young Tuxedo Brass Band playing dirges behind a horse-drawn hearse. After a brief ceremony at the tomb, Antoinette raised her index finger and gently brought it down, the traditional sign that the spirit of the deceased has been cut free from earthly concerns. Then, thousands of revelers on the streets joined mourners for the "second line," the joyful march to upbeat music, to the Mother-in-Law Lounge.

That was not the end for Ernie. Every November first, two hundred or so family members and fans gather at the Duval tomb. "We have wine and cheese," said Twichell, "and tell our favorite Ernie stories." One of them is surely the kind of divine irony much loved in New Orleans: Not long after Ernie K-Doe died, his real-life mother-in-law, Antoinette's mother, passed away. She had lived with the K-Does for many years, and both of them cared for her as she slowly succumbed to Alzheimer's disease. His mother-in-law is now buried next to the singer in the Duval tomb. ✄

karen carpenter
March 2, 1950–February 4, 1983

RIGHT: *The singer's brother, Richard, had her remains moved from this lavish crypt.*

OPPOSITE PAGE: *Carpenter's remains now reside in a family mausoleum near Richard's home.*

*I*n the rock & roll pantheon of overdoses, asphyxiations, plane crashes, and gunshots, Karen Carpenter's death is a bizarre change of pace: She died of a heart attack as a result of Ipecac poisoning. Her life seemed fine when the wholesome Carpenters – Karen and her pianist brother Richard – hit the scene in 1969. They were the anti-Stones: Their lyrics were squeaky clean, their warm harmonies saccharine. Smash singles like "We've Only Just Begun" and "Rainy Days and Mondays," eight gold albums, three Grammys, an Oscar, and a string of TV specials testified to their vast popularity.

In the late 1970s, Karen Carpenter, who had apparently read a review suggesting she was chubby, began to lose weight. The five-foot-three singer became anorexic, using laxatives and vomiting to pare down to a skeletal eighty-three pounds. Work with a psychotherapist seemed to eventually control the disease. By 1982, she had stabilized at a healthy 108 pounds. Secretly though, she was using Ipecac, an over-the-counter medication found in many medicine chests that is used to induce vomiting after an accidental poisoning. If taken repeatedly over time, though, the drug can cause irreversible heart damage. Thus, Carpenter's heart eventually gave out. She fell to the floor of her closet at her parents' Downey, California, home while getting dressed. Ironically, she and her mother were to go clothes shopping that day because of her weight gain. Rescue workers and Richard, who lived around the corner, were called, but it was too late.

Dionne Warwick, Herb Alpert, and pal Olivia Newton-John were among the seven hundred mourners at Downey United Methodist Church. Karen's pastor and friend the Reverend Charles A. Neal talked of the "spontaneous outpouring of love and grief for one of God's truly talented and gifted daughters." She was buried in a spectacular tomb at Forest Lawn Cemetery in Cypress, California. Above the altarlike crypt, which later held her father's remains, was a large painting of the Madonna and child. It was not her final resting place, however. The singer, who became a poster girl for eating disorders with the 1988 TV movie *The Karen Carpenter Story*, was moved some sixty-five miles to Pierce Brothers Valley Oaks Memorial Park in 2003. Richard also had the bodies of their parents reinterred in the mausoleum, nearer to his new home. ❧

ray charles
September 23, 1930–June 10, 2004

Clint Eastwood, B.B. King, Willie Nelson, Stevie Wonder, Glen Campbell, Little Richard: The array of notables among the twelve hundred funeral attendees in Los Angeles' First African Methodist Episcopal Church told the story of Ray Charles's peripatetic genius. He was the king of crossover, mastering R&B, rock, pop, country, and jazz. He even showed up on a TV commercial for Diet Pepsi in 1990 singing, "You got the right one, baby, *uh-huh!*" He virtually – and controversially – invented soul music with dance-party classics like "What'd I Say" and "I Got a Woman" by blending lusty blues licks and pure gospel call-and-response. He made more than sixty original albums, gave more than ten thousand performances, and collected thirteen Grammys. Twice divorced, he fathered twelve children and had twenty grandchildren at the time of his death from liver disease. Charles passed away at his Beverly Hills home, five days after the death of Ronald Reagan.

Many thought that Charles should, like the president, have had a state funeral, too. The musician's casket was displayed at the Los Angeles Convention Center so that thousands of fans could say farewell. A grand piano stood next to the closed coffin; one of Charles's trademark black and silver jackets draped across the piano bench. At the flower-filled church the next day, both Stevie Wonder and B.B. King performed. Clint Eastwood delivered a eulogy, and Willie Nelson was overcome with emotion after singing "Georgia on My Mind." After the funeral, Charles's cortege swung past his Los Angeles office building and recording studio, where it paused for a moment. The musician was interred in a private ceremony at the lush Inglewood Park Cemetery, where his wall crypt is in the Mausoleum of the Golden West. Actors Cesar Romero and Betty Grable are also buried there. Accolades poured in from around the world lauding the man and his music. But shortly before he died, Charles told his autobiography collaborator David Ritz, "Give credit to the church singers and the bluesmen who I got it from. I got enough credit." ✄

At Charles's funeral, Clint Eastwood spoke and Willie Nelson sang.

HARRY NiLSSON

June 15, 1941–January 15, 1994

At a 1997 House of Blues gig in L.A., Marianne Faithfull told the audience that her singer/songwriter pal Harry Nilsson had died three years earlier of a massive heart attack during dental surgery. When the Northridge earthquake hit the city, she said, his casket at a San Fernando Valley funeral home was swallowed by a fissure in the earth, never to be seen again. She then sang his hit, "Don't Forget Me." Great story. Not true. After Nilsson died of heart failure at the suburban Agoura Hills home he shared with his wife, Una, and their seven children, a better joke circulated among his close friends. When George Harrison, Van Dyke Parks, ex-Monkee Mickey Dolenz, and ELO's Jeff Lynne felt the aftershocks of the previous day's devastating quake, they kidded that it was Harry, discovering that there were no bars in Heaven.

As a young computer processor for a bank, Nilsson began writing songs for Phil Spector.

His career took off in the mid-1960s, with hits for the Monkees ("Cuddly Toy") and Three Dog Night ("One"). Ironically, his own 1969 smash, "Everybody's Talkin'," the *Midnight Cowboy* theme song, was written by reclusive folkie Fred Neil. Nonetheless, the Beatles called Nilsson their favorite American songwriter, and during John Lennon's Yoko-less sojourn in L.A. in the mid-1970s, he and Nilsson recorded some rock standards and drank much. A practiced raconteur, Nilsson told his own eerie death tale – he owned the London apartment in which the Who's Keith Moon and Mama Cass Elliot had died four years apart. After Nilsson suffered a heart attack in 1993, he went to work in earnest, finishing an album just three days before he died. He is buried in Pierce Brothers Valley Oaks Memorial Park in Thousand Oaks, where Karen Carpenter also rests. ✀

The singer/songwriter was buried in California around the time of a major earthquake.

HARRY NILSSON

Beloved Husband, Father, Brother, and Friend

June 15, 1941 - January 15, 1994

"Remember..."

The Band

RICHARD MANUEL
April 3, 1943–March 4, 1986

RICK DANKO
December 29, 1942–December 10, 1999

RIGHT: *Canadian keyboardist Manuel is buried in Ontario.*

OPPOSITE PAGE: *The Woodstock grave of countryman Danko remains minimally marked.*

The Band, the legendary roots-rock quintet that became known as Bob Dylan's most prominent backing group, called it quits in 1976 after a decade on the road. Before its farewell concert in San Francisco, documented in Martin Scorsese's *The Last Waltz*, the group had recorded such memorable tracks as "The Weight," "The Night They Drove Old Dixie Down," and "Stage Fright," inspiring fellow musicians like Eric Clapton, among others, with their artistry.

Farewells in rock, though, are often preludes to reunions; the Band, sans lead guitarist Robbie Robertson, hit the road again in 1983. Three years later, after a performance at the Cheek to Cheek Lounge in Winter Park, Florida, pianist/vocalist Richard Manuel stopped by drummer Levon Helm's Quality Inn room. "He sat on the edge of my bed and talked about songs and people," said Helm. "That was the last time I saw him." Around 3:00 a.m., Manuel looped a plain black belt around

his neck, tied the other end around the shower curtain rod in his room, and hanged himself. He left no note. The forty-two-year-old, who had attempted to beat his hard drinking and drugging, had traces of alcohol and cocaine in his system. At his hometown funeral in Stratford, Ontario, Manuel's widow Arlie, ex-wife Jane, their two children, and dozens of relatives and friends listened as the Band's organist Garth Hudson played a Manuel favorite, Dylan's "I Shall Be Released."

Touring, which Robertson once called "a goddamn impossible way of life," took its toll on the Band's bassist, their tenor vocalist, and songwriter Rick Danko. Two years before Danko died of unknown causes at his home near Woodstock, New York, the Canadian was found guilty of colluding to smuggle heroin into Japan while on tour there. "I hope very much that you quit drugs, rehabilitate yourself, and start playing music again soon," the judge in a Chiba court said as he delivered a suspended sentence. "I've been drug-free for three months, so that's a start," said Danko. Drugs hadn't been such a hindrance in the 1960s, though, when Danko famously rented a pink house outside Woodstock where the group recorded its hit debut, *Music From Big Pink*. Danko made two solo albums and reunited with the Band in the 1980s. His grave in Woodstock Cemetery, adjacent to that of his teenage son, carries only a temporary, plastic marker. Fans still find it, however. On a recent day, they had left poignant mementos: a small Canadian flag and a Mr. Goodbar. ✄

BON SCOTT
July 9, 1946–February 19, 1980

On each anniversary of AC/DC frontman Bon Scott's death, security is tightened at Australia's Freemantle Cemetery. A quarter century on, the gravel-voiced singer still draws crowds. The anthems of the heavy-metal bad boys focused on sex, damnation, and drinking, and Scott gained a fervid following by practicing what he preached. A year after AC/DC's breakthrough platinum album *Highway to Hell* hit record bins, Scott set off on his last pub crawl. The down-under outfit had settled in London to record their next album, and Scott spent the night of February 18 pounding scotch with pal Alistair Kinnear. When Kinnear parked at his 67 Overhill Road home, in South London, in the wee hours, he couldn't wake Scott. So he left him in the car to sleep it off. When Kinnear went to his car to check on Scott the next day, he found the AC/DC vocalist dead, choked on his own vomit. Rumors floated about drug abuse and murder plots, but the coroner's report said the cause was simply "acute alcohol poisoning" and ruled it "death by misadventure."

Scott's body was cremated and shipped to Australia. His ashes were interred in Freemantle's sprawling public memorial park, where he remains something of a celebrity. Scott's is the most-visited site; the office and coffee shop display maps pointing the way to his marker, which has been replaced several times due to theft. Empty bottles are the favored tokens left at the plot, but Scott was honored in a different way in the 2004 Australian comedy feature *Thunderstruck*: It follows a group of friends making their way across the Outback to bury a pal next to the singer. ✄

RIGHT: *The AC/DC frontman's memorial bench is a cemetery favorite.*

OPPOSITE PAGE: *The marker of Scott's grave has been stolen several times.*

IN LOVING MEMORY OF
BON SCOTT
LEAD SINGER OF
THE ROCK GROUP AC/DC
THIS SEAT WAS DONATED
BY HIS FAMILY

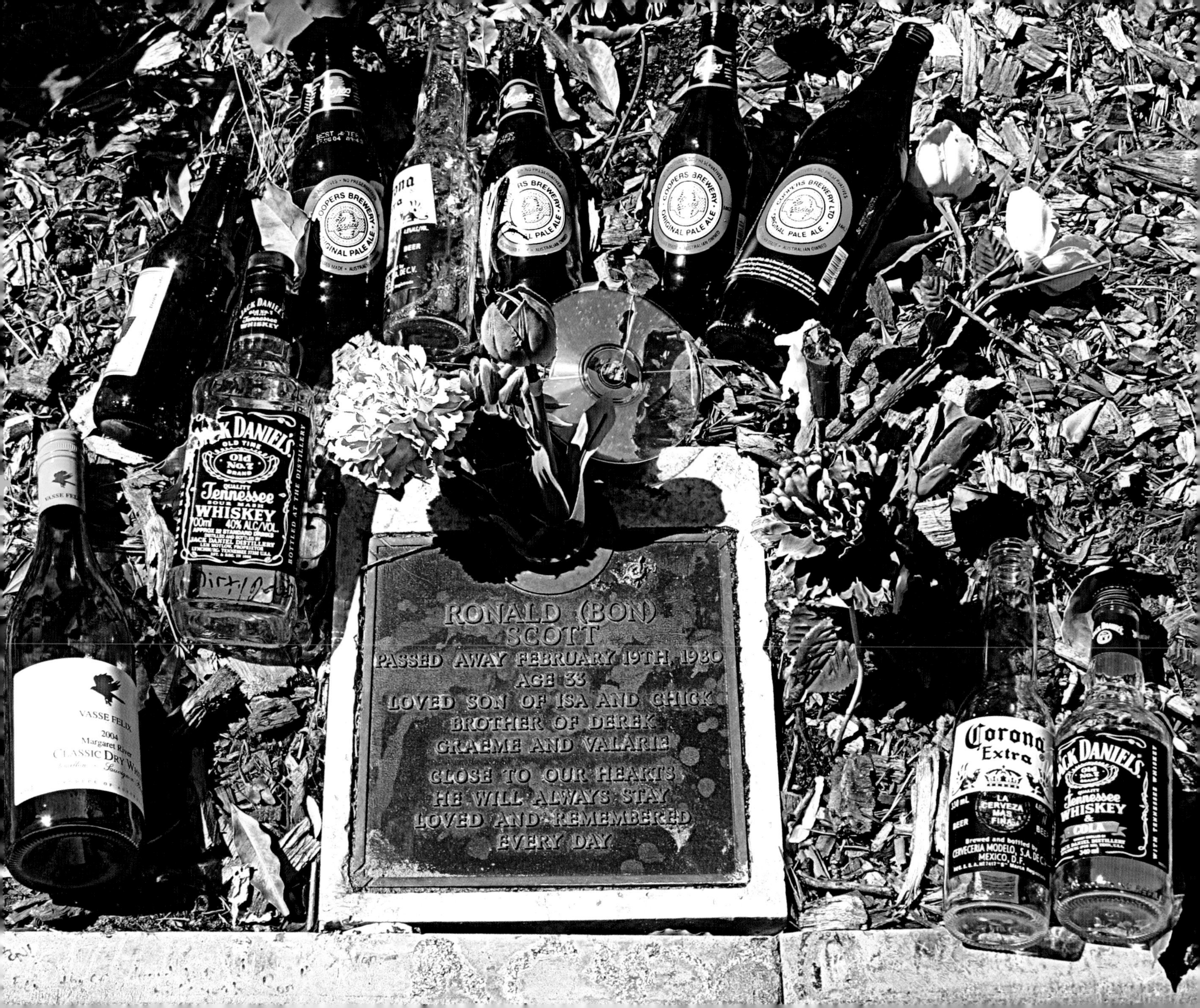
RONALD (BON)
SCOTT
PASSED AWAY FEBRUARY 19TH, 1980
AGE 33
LOVED SON OF ISA AND CHICK
BROTHER OF DEREK
GRAEME AND VALARIE
CLOSE TO OUR HEARTS
HE WILL ALWAYS STAY
LOVED AND REMEMBERED
EVERY DAY
COOPERS BREWERY
ORIGINAL PALE ALE
JACK DANIEL'S
Old No.7
Tennessee
WHISKEY
VASSE FELIX
2004
Margaret River
Corona
Extra
JACK DANIEL'S
Tennessee
WHISKEY
&
COLA

BOB marLey
February 6, 1945–May 11, 1981

*I*n death, Bob Marley has become the Elvis of the Caribbean. He pioneered a musical genre that reached a global audience, winning an ocean of accolades. Like the man from Memphis, Marley's life morphed to legend; his pronouncements to prophecy. And like the King, the Jamaican singer's end was poignantly mundane. Marley hurt his toe playing pickup soccer in France during a 1977 tour. The wound wouldn't heal and eventually turned out to be cancerous. Amputation was the standard treatment, but Marley refused – such surgery was proscribed by his Rastafarian religion. While jogging in Central Park in 1980, Marley collapsed. The malignancy had spread to his lungs, stomach, and brain. He had radiation treatments at Memorial Sloan Kettering Hospital and sought a cure at the German clinic of Dr. Josef Issels, a controversial cancer specialist, but to no avail. As he neared the end, Marley wanted to return to Jamaica but only made it as far as Miami, where he died.

His home country came to a stunned halt. With anthems of love and social action like "No Woman, No Cry," "Get Up, Stand Up," and "Exodus," Marley had galvanized Jamaica's underclass, and his albums had earned $190 million, about ten percent of the island's gross domestic product. The Jamaican parliament adjourned for ten days, and more than 150,000 people, the largest gathering in the nation's history, filed by his casket at the National Heroes Arena in Kingston, the island's capital. Beside him in his coffin were his well-worn Bible and his red Fender Stratocaster. Marley's famous dreadlocks had fallen out due to radiation treatments, but his wife Rita had saved them and wove them into a wig for his service. At his funeral, attended by the nation's current and former prime ministers, Marley's group the Wailers performed,

and his mother, Cedella Booker, sang one of the last songs he wrote, "Coming in From the Cold."

Marley rests at Nine Miles, the rustic, mountainside compound seventy-five miles from Kingston, where he grew up. While it lacks the glitz of Graceland, many elements are similar. The site is owned and operated by the singer's family, as is Elvis's estate, and cheery guides (in this case Rastafarians) lead visitors to the sights: the tiny stone cabin where Marley was born; his meditation spot, called Zion Rock; and, of course, the bustling gift shop. The last stop is the whitewashed mausoleum. "No pictures inside please, mon," instructs the escort. Marley is interred in a cement sarcophagus, surrounded by trinkets, notes, and a few generous joints left by fans.

Like Elvis, Marley, whose February 6 birthday became a Jamaican national holiday in 1991, has done well indeed since his demise. In 2004, the reggae king made ninth place on the *Forbes* magazine top-earning dead celebrities list, with a seven-million-dollar post-mortem income. Marley's posthumous greatest-hits album, *Legend*, has sold more than twenty million copies to date, and his family has expanded the business. The singer's son Robbie recently opened Vintage Marley, a flagship Miami store offering CDs, licensed Catch a Fire Clothing, Bob Marley Footwear, and Zion Roots wear. More is on the way. Rita Marley unveiled an ambitious 2005 schedule to celebrate what would have been the Rastaman's sixtieth year. A Gala Memorial Concert featuring Lauryn Hill and Anjélique Kidjo took place in Ethiopia, home of the Rastafarian religion, and a CD of previously unreleased material was issued. Those worn out by the whirl of activities can soon relax: A Marley Resort and Spa is scheduled to open in the Bahamas in 2006. ✶

RIGHT AND ABOVE: *The Rastaman's tomb is housed in a two-story building.*

FOLLOWING PAGES: *Painted stones remember Bob outside his mausoleum; the stone cottage where Marley was born.*

146

DEE DEE RAMONE
September 18, 1951–June 5, 2002

JOEY RAMONE
May 19, 1951–April 15, 2001

JOHNNY RAMONE
October 8, 1948–September 15, 2004

RIGHT: *A message from a fan left at Joey's grave.*

OPPOSITE PAGE: *Joey's resting place is in Lyndhurst, New Jersey.*

End of the Century

With their motorcycle jackets, Prince Valiant haircuts, and rapid-fire thrashing on songs like "Now I Wanna Sniff Some Glue" and "Teenage Lobotomy," the Ramones were the godfathers of punk rock. The group, which took its name from Paul Ramon, an early pseudonym of Paul McCartney's, never had a gold studio album, never changed their unpretentious tune to please MTV or to score on the charts, yet they influenced artists from the Sex Pistols to Green Day. The Ramones, said E Street Band guitarist and actor Little Steven Van Zandt, "were the most important band that never made it." The members of the group, which formed in 1974, could have been cut down young by the toxic perils of downtown celebrity. But they defied the odds and burned their three-chord anthems for twenty-three years, on more than a dozen albums, before finally unplugging their amps in 1996. What sustained them and protected them, said filmmaker and friend Rachel Amodeo, was that "they were just regular guys from Queens."

"Regular," however, was no defense against the inevitable. In 2001, vocalist Joey Ramone (né Jeffery Hyman), announced that he was undergoing treatment for lymphoma. He eventually weakened, and, as he lay in New York-Presbyterian Hospital on Good Friday, he received visitors and phone calls from such admirers as U2's Bono. On Easter Sunday, with Joey's family gathered at his bedside, his brother Mickey Leigh put U2's *All That You Can't Leave Behind* on the CD player. By the time it ended, Joey was dead. At the Jewish graveyard at Hillside Cemetery in Lyndhurst, New Jersey, his funeral was attended by, among others, the band's original drummer, Tommy Ramone (Tommy Erdelyi), and Joan Jett. Joey's old pal Deborah Harry of Blondie saw the spires of Manhattan in the distance and said, "At least he has a good view."

After Joey's death, the tension that had plagued the group became public. Early on, straight-edge guitarist Johnny Ramone (né John Cummings) had chafed at Joey's erratic, rock star nonchalance, while Joey seethed when his girlfriend Linda Danielle went off with Johnny, eventually marrying him. The acrimony never waned. "I was in California," Johnny told *Rolling Stone* when asked if he attended Joey's funeral. "I wasn't going to travel all the way to New York. But I wouldn't have gone anyway. I wouldn't want him coming to my funeral, and I wouldn't want to hear from him if I were dying."

When the Ramones were inducted into the Rock and Roll Hall of Fame, in March 2002, Dee Dee Ramone (né Douglas Glenn Colvin), always the ultimate punk, cheerfully told the crowd, "I'd like to congratulate and thank myself." Although he had always been the band's wild child, his debilitating drug use seemed years in the past. In a 1991

Douglas Glenn Colvin

Sept. 18, 1951
June 5, 2002

DEE DEE RAMONE

O.K...I gotta go now

ABOVE: *Dee Dee's Hollywood grave is emblazoned with the group's "seal."*

LEFT: *Douglas Glenn Colvin will always be remembered as Dee Dee Ramone.*

OPPOSITE PAGE: *A well-known Ramones line is inscribed on Dee Dee's tombstone.*

Nicolas Cage and Lisa Marie Presley helped unveil Johnny's statue, near Dee Dee's grave.

interview for the documentary film *Hey Is Dee Dee Home*, he regretfully said of his infamous drug-scoring song "Chinese Rock," "I feel like I became some kind of heroin guru." Apparently he wasn't finished. His wife Barbara found fifty-year-old Dee Dee dead in their Hollywood home of what was determined to be an "accidental overdose" of heroin.

Two years later, Johnny, a stalwart conservative and Ronald Reagan admirer, succumbed to the prostate cancer he had battled for seven years. His final months were mellow. He retired from performing in 1996, saying, "I just want to hang out and watch horror movies." He died at his Los Angeles home, and his remains were cremated and returned to Linda. Four months later, she unveiled a life-size bronze statue of the guitarist strumming his Mosrite, not far from Dee Dee's grave at Hollywood Forever Cemetery. Actor Nicolas Cage and the lone surviving original Ramone, Tommy, joined hundreds of fans at the ceremony. Johnny was inspired to commission the sculpture after watching the pomp and circumstance of Reagan's state funeral on TV. But he balked at the hundred-thousand-dollar price of the piece by Wayne Toth, who also creates special-effects makeup for films like *House of 1000 Corpses*. Finally, thoughts of his legacy — and a little competitive spirit — won out. Said Linda, "He wanted people, the fans, to come from all over the world and get to see it. He wanted it to be bigger than Jim Morrison's grave." ✁

Fans leave Ramone doll parts on Joey's tombstone.

∾ acknowledgments ∾

For their generous help with research into the text: In Paris, Bryan Alexander, Peter Mikelbank, and Cathy Nolan; in England, Nigel Davies; in the South, Peter Guralnick, Skip Henderson, Candace Oakley, and Phil Walden; in New York, Rachel Amodeo; in Hollywood, Kelly Spencer; in New Orleans, Antoinette K-Doe and Anna Ross Twichell; and in Iowa, Ken Paquette. And thanks to Corky Smith for his priceless guidance.

For their invaluable assistance with photographs: In New York, thank you Jen Lombardo, consulting photo editor and researcher; and thank you Shelley Dowell and Rashida Morgan; in New York, Pennyslvania, New Jersey, Los Angeles, and England, Veronica Stephens for her dedication to the project and expert navigational skills; in the U.K., Bruce and Lynne Prochnik and Ian Cook. Thanks to Olympus Imaging for the loan of the C-8080; Wendie Demuth, and Chris Sluka.

And hats off to our fearless editor Holly George-Warren, designer Ellen Nygaard, managing editor Nina Pearlman, researcher Rachel X. Weissman, copy editor Robin Aigner, and Jann S. Wenner and his marvelous crew at Wenner Books: Bob Wallace, Kate Rockland, John Dragonetti, KellyAnn Kwiatek, and Linda Pitt.

– *J.D. Reed and Maddy Miller*

OPPOSITE PAGE: *A lipstick kiss on Randy Rhoads's tomb*

∾ about the authors ∾

J.D. Reed was raised in Wayne, Michigan, which happens to be the final resting place of R&B heart-throb Jackie Wilson ("Lonely Teardrops"). He published three books of poems and taught creative writing at the University of Massachusetts in Amherst until he became weary of signing add-drop cards. In 1975, he signed on as a writer at Time Inc., and did not leave the Time-Life Building for twenty-six years, working at *Sports Illustrated*, *Time*, and *People* magazines. He "retired" to central New Jersey in 2001, where he and his wife, Christine, raised three daughters. J.D. Reed has made absolutely no arrangements for his own grave or tombstone.

Maddy Miller had her first rock & roll moment in 1965, when she was in the studio audience for the Beatles' first appearance on *The Ed Sullivan Show*. A native New Yorker, she was raised on photography. Her father, Dan Miller, started his career at *Look* magazine, as did Maddy. His photograph of John Belushi's Martha's Vineyard grave appears in this book. Maddy is currently a photo editor at *People* magazine, where she has worked on many special issues including *The World's Most Beautiful People* and *The Sexiest Man Alive*. In addition to her role as coauthor of *Stairway to Heaven*, she contributed many of the photographs.

OPPOSITE PAGE: *A detail from the stone of the Supremes' Florence Ballard*

∾ PHOTOGRAPHY CREDITS ∾

Gravesites:

Photographs by **Maddy Miller** (1, 3, 10–13, 19, 22–23, 31, 40–49, 54, 56–57, 63, 65, 67, 72, 74, 76, 80–83, 86–92, 97–99, 110, 122–123, 132–133, 137–139, 148–151, 153–154, 158)

Alan Bean (2, 16, 18); **Roger Scruton** (5, 15, 30, 77–79); **Sarah Kunstler and Emily Kunstler** (6, 11, 20–21, 58–59, 108–109, 134–135); **AP** (8); **Ann States** (14, 28–29, 130–131); **Marianne Morf**/*Clear Lake Reporter* (17); **Quinton P. Young III** (24–27, 94); **Thomas Boggan** (32–33); **Michelle Campbell, ©2005 ARS, New York/DACS, London** (34–37); **John Pearson Wright/ Time Life Pictures/Getty** (35, top right); **Steve Brown**/*The Sun Runner* (38–39); **Lee Celano** (38, top right); **J.D. Reed** (50); **Tamara Reynolds** (51, 102–104, 107); **Mike Brown/Getty** (52); **Mario Tama/Getty** (53); **Brian Widdis** (55, 62, 93, 95–96, 120–121, 156); **George Tuley** (60–61); **Moritz Hoffmann** (64); **Erik C. Pendzich** (66); **Jen Lombardo** (68); **David Berkwitz** (71); **Ian Cook** (73, 75); **John Huffer** (84–85); **Holly George-Warren** (101);

Dave Cruz (105); **Al Rendon** (106); **Hitoshi Sasaki** (111); **Mike Hettwer** (113–115, 118, 160); **Dan Miller** (117, 119); **Kent Jennings Brockwell** (124–127); **Les Duggins Sr.** (128–129); **Jim McHugh** (136); **Brian Hassett** (140); **Ben Caswell** (141); **Nick Fairweather** (142–143); **Rasheed Girvan** (145–147); **Evans Ward** (152)

Artists:

Michael Ochs Archives (Richardson and Valens, 16; 22–23; 26; Oakley, 28; 34; 40–41; 48; 54–56; 62–63; Harrison, 66; 72; 76; 81; Elliot and Phillips, 82; 86; 91–92; Ballard, 96; 98; Carter Family and Cash with Carter Cash, 100; 104–108; Smith, 110; 111; Wolf, Waters, and Dixon, 112; 116; Tyner and Smith, 120; Nolan, 122; Van Zant, Steve Gaines, Wilkson, and Collins, 124; Toy Caldwell, 128; 132–134; 139; Danko, 140); **John Beecher/Michael Ochs Archives** (Holly, 16); **Robert Johnson Studio Portrait: Hooks Bros., Memphis, c. 1935, ©1989 Delta Haze Corporation. All Rights Reserved. Used By Permission** (24); **Michael Dobo/Michael Ochs Archives** (Allman, 28; Lennon, 66); **Astrid Kirchherr/Star File** (Sutcliffe, 30); **Harry Goodwin/Rex** (Jones, 30); **Harry Goodwin/Michael Ochs Archives** (32, 90, 136); **Ginny Winn/Michael Ochs Archives** (38); **Gary Gershoff/Retna** (42); **Keith Morris/Michael Ochs Archives** (44); **Doc Pele/Stills/Retna** (50); **Dave Allocca/Rex** (57); **Stephanie Chernikowski/Michael Ochs Archives** (58); **Larry Busacca/ Retna** (60); **Nikpop/Redferns/Retna** (64); **Richard Mann/Retna** (65); **David Corio/Michael Ochs Archives** (70); **Chris Foster/Retna** (77); **Robert Knight/Retna** (78); **Rex** (80, 138); **Steve Eichner/Retna** (84); **Ian Showell/Keystone/Getty** (87); **Austin Young** (88); **Dezo Hoffmann/Rex** (Wells, 96); **Fitzroy Barrett/Retna** (99); **Daniel Kramer/Camera Press/Retna** (Joplin, 110); **P. Felix/Getty** (Murcia, Thunders, and Kane, 122); **Getty** (Cassie Gaines, 124; 142); **Jon Sievert/Michael Ochs Archives** (Tommy Caldwell, 128); **David Hogan/Getty** (130); **Frank Driggs Collection/Getty** (Manuel, 140); **Kim Gottlieb-Walker/Michael Ochs Archives** (144); **Kees Tabak/Sunshine/Retna** (148)

OPPOSITE PAGE: *Details on a music lover's grave*

A sentiment on the headstone of Muddy Waters